D0040369

Michael Marshall

JUST LIKE HIM!

- The Bible Reading Fellowship was founded 'to encourage the systematic and intelligent reading of the Bible, to emphasize its spiritual message and to take advantage of new light shed on Holy Scripture'.

- Over the years the Fellowship has proved a trustworthy guide for those who want an open, informed and contemporary approach to the Bible. It retains a sense of the unique authority of Scripture as a prime means by which God communicates.

- As an ecumenical organization, the Fellowship embraces all Christian traditions and its readers are to be found in most parts of the world.

MICHAEL MARSHALL

Just Like Him!

The Passion of Christ
in the
Old Testament

the bible reading fellowship

The Bible Reading Fellowship
Warwick House
25 Buckingham Palace Road
London SW1W 0PP

First published 1989

© Michael Marshall 1989

All rights reserved. No part of this publication may be reproduced, stored in a retrieval system, or transmitted, in any form or by any means, electronic, mechanical, photocopying, recording or otherwise, without the prior permission of the publishers.

Bible quotations are taken from the Revised Standard Version, copyright 1973 by Division of Christian Education of the National Council of the Churches of Christ in the USA.

Marshall, Michael, *1936–*
    Just Like Him!: the passion of Christ in the Old Testament.
    1. Bible — Critical Studies
    I. Title II. Bible Reading Fellowship 220.6

    ISBN 0–900164–79–4

Back cover photograph: South London Press.

Printed and designed by Bocardo Press Ltd, Didcot, England.

CONTENTS

Dedicated to

Paul Jobson

a wonderful friend and colleague in the gospel of Jesus Christ, one of God's truly J-shaped servants.

'Do you not know that all of us who have been baptized into Christ Jesus were baptized into his death? We were buried therefore with him by baptism into death, so that as Christ was raised from the dead by the glory of the Father, we too might walk in newness of life.' (Romans 6:3–4)

A J-shaped prayer for Lent

Father of mankind,
who gave your only begotten Son
to take upon himself the form of a servant
and to be obedient even to death on a cross:
give us the same mind that was in Christ Jesus
that, sharing his humility,
we may come to be with him in his glory;
who is alive and reigns with you and the Holy Spirit,
one God, now and for ever. Amen.

(*Alternative Service Book 1980*: Pentecost 10)

PREFACE

Any book is a labour of love! Writing a book is necessarily a team effort involving many others besides the one whose name appears on the cover. In the first place I am grateful to the Bible Reading Fellowship for inviting me to write this book for their Lent Course. It is hard to over-estimate the importance of the Fellowship internationally in bringing the scriptures into the life of the churches, so making them accessible for young and old, for laity and for clergy. It is my earnest hope that this book will have some part to play in helping many to read the scriptures prayerfully and with expectation throughout the season of Lent, Holy week and Easter.

My gratitude must also be expressed to Georgia Streett of the the Anglican Institute who helped at the outset to forge the outline of the book. Mary Baddeley produced the bulk of the typescript swiftly and accurately and under a great time constraint. I am grateful to her for this as for so many other ways in which she has supported and helped me in my ministry over many years.

I am grateful also to the bishop, clergy and laity of the Diocese of Southern Carolina, USA for the opportunity to test out the thesis of this book at a conference convened by Temperance Parker in that diocese in 1988.

✝ Michael Marshall
Anglican Institute, St Louis USA

INTRODUCING
GOD'S J-SHAPED PEOPLE

Joel: Jacob: Joshua: Joseph: Jonah: Job: Jeremiah

Who are these people?

'Then one of the elders addressed me, saying, "Who are these, clothed in white robes, and whence have they come?" I said to him, "Sir, you know." And he said to me, "These are they, who have come out of the great tribulation"'' (Revelation 7:13–14). Put another way — these people are people who have been *through* it! They are God's 'Red-Sea people', with a story to tell and to retell of what they have been through — their 'great tribulation.'

The Bible (especially the Old Testament) is not really a religious book in quite the same way that many people would describe a religious book. Indeed, St Augustine of Hippo, after shopping around the supermarkets of other religious options in his day, with their sophisticated and highly 'spiritual' flavour, found the stories, especially of the Old Testament, highly irreligious, bloodthirsty and too down-to-earth by half. The book was not sufficiently 'spiritual' for Augustine before his conversion.

For the Bible is not a 'religious' or 'spiritual' book in quite that way. The Bible is in fact the record of people's lives which have been reshaped by events — strange events, often events in which they had very little say. They are people whose lives have either individually or collectively been 'struck' by God. The blow has frequently been painful and often traumatic. It has turned their lives around however, so that it sometimes seems as though they are facing themselves coming in the wrong direction! Yet there is a definite family likeness about all these people. It is almost as though they have a spiritually genetic similarity, not only in the stories which they tell, but in the profiles of the lives which they have lived.

Who on earth are they? They could all be forgiven for having had at some point in their lives, what is nowadays called an identity crisis. Yet you do not solve an identity crisis by endless introspection, but rather by persistent retrospection. You need to look back just as much as you need to look in. You look back at those who have gone before you and you begin to identify with them. In other words you discover your identity from those with whom you identify.

So this book traces the stories (many of them well-known) of the lives of seven Old Testament characters who are, in theological terms, what we call 'salvation figures'. They are not especially good people (and certainly not particularly nice people) — take Jacob, for one example. Neither are many of them especially impressive people, by our standards — take Job or Jonah. Yet as we persist in reflecting upon their lives, there is in fact a family likeness: their profiles are a similar shape. In a word, these people have been clearly chosen by God.

J-shaped people

In this book we call them J-shaped people: people put down by life and raised up by God. They are often outcasts who have ended up being called in, 'out of the cold', into the inner and hidden counsels of God: Joel, Jacob, Joshua, Joseph, Jonah, Job and Jeremiah. They have all kinds of traits in common. In the first place they are clearly people of contradiction: they are weak men who have been made strong. It often seems as though it was only at the end of their lives, that real life began. They are unfairly and unjustly put down and yet amazingly raised up beyond our wildest imaginings. Emptied of self, they seem strangely free to live for others: they genuinely end up loving their enemies. Clearly their lives are not fulfilled by human standards and yet they are also equally clearly filled full of love, of life and of grace. Furthermore they are a passionate people who always seem to be getting out of their depth, involved in and undergoing strange, painful and terrible experiences without finally going under. Often, almost at the last minute, their lives are reversed and they are distinctively and amazingly raised up. They are peculiarly J-shaped!

The danger is that if you read the record of these lives in the semi-chronological order in which they are presented in the Old Testament, you are in danger of writing them off as a rag-bag of remnants and oddments from some strange, religious 'soap-operas'. There is much similarity between everybody and there are many things they have in common. Yet, the stories we read here only make sense if we read them back to front — rather in the same way that their lives seem to have been lived, namely, upside down and inside out. For essentially this book only makes sense in the end, as being the record of lives which were J-shaped, and as signs of contradiction. In another sense this book is the record of one particular Person whose life was supremely J-shaped — namely Jesus. He shows us how to live the divine life as a man, in this strange-shaped and perverted world. We shall however probably not recognize Jesus for who he truly is, unless we begin (as he instructed those bewildered disciples on the road to Emmaus to begin), 'with Moses and all the prophets'. Then we begin to discern the features which all these J-shaped people have in common — they are the features of salvation figures.

The passion of Christ will only make sense to us if we relate it to all the 'passions' of all the other J-shaped people of the scriptural record. In turn the 'passions' of these strange, shadowy characters from the Old Testament only really come alive when their stories resonate with, and in the end are seen to belong with, the one great story — the story of Jesus in his passion, death and resurrection.

Three stories

Yet there is a further, third and thrilling dimension. There is a place where three ways meet and converge — for it is as though there are three stories to tell as the scriptures come fully alive in three-dimensional relief and lift off the page intruding into our world, and into *our* stories — as they become truly contemporary. The church is the new Israel, called by God out of the slavery of sin, through the waters of baptism and into the land of Promise and Gift. The contemporary Christian pilgrim often has an identity crisis. Who am I? What is a Christian? St Paul would be quite adamant in his reply: it might go something like this: 'You are his; you belong to him of course. His life in you and your life *in Christ*.' Or, in the words of Jesus, 'You did not choose me, but I chose you' (John 15:16).

For there is in fact a third 'story' to recall. It is my story — a strange story indeed. In all honesty I find that story to be the record of a person of strange contradictions and inversions. It is as though I do not quite fit into the world's scheme of things. I frequently feel as though I am the wrong shape, like 'a square peg in a round hole,' as we say. Yet I have a story to tell, and just from time to time it seems to resonate rather strikingly with many of those other strange stories I read about in the lives of other J-shaped people in the Old Testament. When I look at their lives they are often in the same sort of complexity as my own and I begin to see a strange kind of family likeness. In some ways I often feel just like Jonah — fleeing from God. Yes, perhaps I am just a bit like them, as — dare I say it? — they are all just a bit like Jesus. Of course it all depends how you see it and other people might dismiss my conjectures as fanciful and even absurd. But somehow in all of this I find myself sticking to a great tradition — and yet I end up being even more aware that somehow this whole topsy-turvy world of J-shaped people is 'sticking' to me. No — I don't *understand* the scriptures, yet they retain a strange power to haunt me.

So it is almost as though there are three stories. There is 'his-story': that's the easiest to relate and often great fun. The stories of the Old Testament are such good yarns, as we say, about these J-shaped people and they are told so well.

Then of course there is the 'old, old story'! 'Tell me the old, old story, of Jesus and his love.' That's the story which the church delights to tell and recall every time it convenes. The pre-occupation with that story is not unreasonable. For the task of this church is to show forth the shape of Christ's death and resurrection and so *impress* that shape upon people that something of the shape and form of resurrection — ultimate reality — breaks through even now into our shadowy world. The church's task is literally to show forth his death and resurrection 'until he comes again' " (1 Corinthians 11:26).

Yet if it all stops there, there is something flat and two-dimensional about the world of faith and about the proclamation of the church. 'This is your life!' That was the title of a television programme which used to tell the stories of famous people's lives. At the end of the programme as the producer completed the story and brought it up to date, he would turn, with book in hand and say in words of exclamation and proclamation — 'This is your life'. He handed to the person concerned a large and well-bound volume and record of the life-story of the unfortunate victim chosen for this kind of notoriety.

So with the scriptures: it is as though in some sense we begin to feel ourselves reading the scriptures in the first person. 'This is *your* life.' We find ourselves as we open the scriptures and read this record faithfully and imaginatively, beginning to say something like, 'Isn't that just like the time when. . .?' For all three stories are in some strange way related: his-story, the Jesus story and my story and furthermore all three converge in *him*. Of course they are blurred at the edges, most surely, yet sufficiently and substantially the three different stories are recognizable as one. The identity kit fits — we are recognized for who we are (by God's grace). It all begins to ring true. It is as though, like the disciples on the Emmaus road, 'our hearts burn within us'. Yes, that is my life. . . 'if I am his, and he is mine for ever'. Dare I say it? It is as though I am part of one great family 'business' — the 'business of heaven' on earth. The family tree stretches through all the other J-shaped people that I find in the record of salvation history in the pages of the Old Testament.

Salvation figures
Of course if it is put like this and left there, it could all sound highly subjective and a bit like a spiritual fantasy. It is not enough just to see ourselves as strange people who seem a little 'touched' — touched, literally and metaphorically. For if that is the point of it all then individualism and pietism will win the day and the rest of the world 'untouched' will be simply thrown on the rubbish heap at the end of history. Happily, however, there is nothing élitist about salvation figures. For the plan of God's salvation is for the whole world. The many are saved by the few: the few are saved by the one. God's 'chosen people' (in the old and the new Israel alike) are not chosen for their own salvation only, but rather to be part in some mysterious way of Christ's whole redeeming act in the history of the whole world. The church, as Archbishop William Temple constantly reminds us, does not exist for itself alone. It exists for those who are not members of it. The 'few' are 'chosen' for

the sake of the 'many' who are 'called' (Matthew 22:14). God touches certain lives — the mystery of election — for the sake of many lives. 'This is my blood which is shed for you and *for many*.'

In the economy of history, revolution and change, it is as though the saints of God are the hinge on which all else turns. Jesus and his J-shaped friends are members of a single body and cell, who lay down their lives for the rest of the world. Of course, the sacrifice of Christ on Calvary is once for all, unique and all-sufficient. Nothing we say must detract from that. We cannot add anything to Christ's sacrifice nor should we try to subtract anything from it. Yet salvation history is the record of those before Christ and after Christ who have been drawn into this one sacrifice — caught up in it all. (That is one of the 'spin-offs' of a full-blooded doctrine of the Incarnation.) Very little of their achievements (if achievement is the right word) has much to do with their own efforts. It is as though they are the first-fruits of a larger harvest beyond even their wildest expectations. Therefore, without those who have gone before us (all these Old Testament heroes) we shall not 'be made perfect' in Christ — the plan of redemption history will not be complete (Hebrews 11:39—40). It is only *together*, incorporated into Christ, that in some sense the whole body of these people begins to make some sense. Together the whole body of Christ is essentially priestly. That means it lives for others — for the rest of the world. Along with Jesus it 'ever liveth to make intercession for' the world (Hebrews 7:25). These J-shaped people are all essentially intercessory men and women who always seem to want to plead the cause of others. They are advocates; they are intercessors; they are priestly in character and in nature. The essential characteristic of God's chosen people is that together in Christ they constitute a priesthood. In the world it is every man for himself— that is the way we've evolved: the survival of the fittest. It is not like that in the kingdom. In the kingdom it has to be, because in the end it will be, everyone for others: each for all and all for each.

Suffering and service
So the shape of revelation history is radically unlike that of evolutionary history: it is *not* straightforward. Perhaps it is rather J-shaped! For the church is not the same as the kingdom. The church points to the kingdom and together with Christ as its spiritual and incarnate head, the church at its best can be the catalyst for the kingdom. So in both Old and New Testament alike, those who are chosen by God to be identified with the redemptive salvation process are in some mysterious way chosen not for privilege but for service; not to experience a massage but to bear a message: to make up that which is still 'lacking in Christ's afflictions for the sake of his body, that is, the church' (Colossians 1:24).

Often J-shaped people's lives are something of a paradox by the world's standards. They are frequently seen as even hypocritical: they seem to bear more than their share of suffering — the kind of suffering which constitutes a real stumbling block to faith in a loving God.

For Christianity does not explain suffering. J-shaped people are a wonderful record, however, of what God can do for the world with unavoidable suffering when it is accepted and truly offered. At the very least, the world is enriched by such suffering: at the most, and at the highest, it was actually saved and redeemed by such suffering.

So there is a mysterious fellowship between Joel, Jacob, Joshua, Joseph, Jonah, Job, Jeremiah, the Jews, Jesus and all the other J-shaped people of the universe. It is significant that Jesus did not stand alone on top of the mountain of Transfiguration in his overview of salvation history. His vision and perspective stretch back to the early days of Moses and Elijah and forward to his own exodus in Jerusalem and beyond. As he reflected upon his 'exodus' and upon the fuller meaning of salvation together with his forthcoming suffering and death, he did so in the company of the caucus of the new Israel (Peter, James and John) and also in the context of the old Israel — Moses and Elijah. The gospel records are at pains to tell us that he spoke with Moses and Elijah (those two strange J-shaped people from the past) and also with Peter, James and John, his J-shaped earthly companions, about the matters of J-shaped history of which the 'exodus' is the most notable of all J-shaped reversals in the Old Testament.

'Since we are surrounded by so great a cloud of witnesses, let us lay aside every weight, and sin which clings so closely, and let us run with perseverance the race that is set before us, looking to Jesus the pioneer and perfecter of our faith' (Hebrews 12:1—2).

Yes, all eyes of history are supremely fixed on him. For all history now turns around him. Yet in the crowd as I look around I think I can recognize the friends of this Jesus — 'Tell me your friends and I will tell you what you are,' we rightly say! Around Jesus there are many others who in some sense are 'just a bit like him' — those other J-shaped people. Like all good pilgrims and travellers, of course, they are telling their tales and their stories. There is a great deal of humour and their stories are very down-to-earth — some might even accuse them of being rather earthy. At some point, possibly, I shall be invited to tell my story — 'This is my story, this is my song'. It will be a little easier now to articulate my story in the context of theirs. Of course I cannot explain everything about myself — perhaps I do not need to do so after all. For along with the others I also have been washed in the blood of the Lamb. That of course is always a great leveller. For all alike have been 'raised up': they have not 'climbed up' some other way (John 10:1). There is no other way. Now at last we know who we are, because finally we know whose we are. We are his, of course. There is a real family likeness between us all — perhaps

13

after all we really were made in his image: not just once in the beginning (our creation) but for a second time (our salvation). So perhaps it is high time we recognized his hand in all of this refusing to be ashamed of it, to apologize for it, nor demanding to understand it all. 'I am not ashamed of the gospel', says St Paul, that supremely J-shaped apostle (Romans 1:16).

Using this book

All together of course it should be admitted that it is rather a strange story. But that is how you have to take it, otherwise you will probably leave it. But take it or leave it, these stories in this book all belong together. The Old Testament only makes sense and has a shape about it if it is seen together with Jesus and the New Testament. Similarly much that Jesus said and did and is, will be lost on us if we take him out of the 'tradition' in which he is truly at home and in which he really belongs. In isolation, individualism makes little sense in the real world.

So for each day of Lent there are three sections. The first question we need to ask ourselves might go something like this: 'What did this story mean when it was told in its own time?' The second question would be something like this: 'Does it resonate with the story of Jesus in his time?' But above all there is a third question: 'Does it ring true today and for ever?' These are not of course three separate and unrelated stories. They belong to a single bold event — the Jesus event. It is to be hoped that in groups you will be led to share 'your story'.

At the beginning of each week there is a section to introduce the figure of the week and some questions for reflection and study as you read over the passages for each day of that week. Therefore this book could be used equally well corporately in a parish, Lenten discussion or Bible study group, and/or individually each day throughout Lent. Biblical passages are deliberately printed out in full so that if the book is taken to work, on a train, or in an aeroplane, the student will only need to carry one book instead of two. The book is deliberately shaped for pilgrims of the resurrection and it is intended to bring us in heart and mind in another year of grace to a yet fuller and deeper understanding of the mystery of the resurrection — the mystery of 'Christ in you, the hope of glory' (Colossians 1:27).

JOEL: THE TRUE RADICAL

WHATEVER the dating of the book of Joel may be (and here as in so many other places, scholars are confused and divided), the *occasion* of the book of Joel is quite clear. The book was occasioned by a devastating locust plague. Those who have never experienced a plague of locusts can hardly imagine the extent of its devastation and destruction. It is a story which fathers tell their children from generation to generation and not unnaturally the story grows with the telling!

> 'Hear this, you aged men,
> give ear, all inhabitants of the land!
> Has such a thing happened in your days,
> or in the days of your fathers?
> Tell your children of it,
> and let your children tell their children,
> and their children another generation.

> What the cutting locust left,
> the swarming locust has eaten.
> What the swarming locust left,
> the hopping locust has eaten,
> and what the hopping locust has left,
> the destroying locust has eaten. . .

> The fields are laid waste
> the ground mourns;
> because the grain is destroyed,
> the wine fails,
> the oil languishes.' (Joel 1:2—4, 10)

For Joel this catastrophic event demands that *we stop and think* — in a word, that we repent. The word repentance is perhaps the most glorious and most positive word in the human vocabulary: it means to stop and think; to have second thoughts, to change one's mind. The wicked Fagin in the musical, *Oliver Twist*, expresses repentance in a mildly humorous way: 'I am reviewing the situation. . .' Yes, that's it precisely. Often in personal stories as well as in the great stories of history, it is the catastrophe which brings us up with a shock and demands that we 'review the situation'.

In AD 410 Rome, the great city of the empire was sacked by the Vandals. The shock waves from that event ran out through the culture and civilization

15

of the ancient world. What is this shattering event saying to us? St Augustine reached for his pen, and wrote about another city — the City of God. He saw the event of the sack of Rome in a different perspective; in a different shape, with a different profile and meaning. Because of what he wrote, ears throughout the ancient world would soon be more tuned to hear reports from the heavenly city whose foundations could never be shaken.

So it is with repentance. The prophet Joel calls upon God's people to see history in a different light. History is not a meaningless, pointless or endless string of events. It has a shape and a purpose. There are turning points which point towards an ultimate meaning which transcends the immediate events of the day. Joel points to such a moment in history and calls it 'the day of the Lord'. He demands that we see the events of our lives and of our history in the light of what is ultimate: that we see passing events and the dust and debris of catastrophies in the light of foundations which can never crumble and which will be standing when all else has fallen. 'Heaven and earth will pass away,' says Jesus, 'but my words will not pass away' (Mark 13:31). It is in the light of what remains standing on the day of the Lord, that we need to reorganize and to rearrange all our priorities. On that day, the first indeed will be last, and the last will be first. Our world will be turned upside down, inside out and back to front. Such is the message, the radical message of Joel.

Each year the church concentrates afresh on the most significant and earth-shattering event of all history — the death and resurrection of Jesus. In the light of that event, all else is changed and the long shadows cast by the light of Easter Day stretch back over six weeks of Lent, challenging our priorities, and demanding that we also in our day 'stop and think': that we 'review' the situation.

For Joel is that kind of radical. He transcends the contemporary. He transcends the contemporary by digging even deeper. That is deliberately a sign of contradiction, for Joel is a J-shaped person. His whole message is J-shaped, truly radical and fundamental in its rejection of evil.

So Joel in his prophecy issues a call to repentance and it is wholly appropriate that such a radical prophet should begin our Lenten course. For the challenge is to stop and think it out all over again: to dig deeper than ever for firm foundations of faith. When we do, we are indeed impressed by the profile of reality. We discover it is a different shape to that which the world tends to idolize. It is the story of how the good news can be discovered all among the bad news ('the years which the locusts have devoured'). Bad Friday becomes Good Friday. The 'dead-ends' of our desires become the new beginnings of possibilities beyond our wildest imaginings. We begin to become J-shaped people as our minds and our outlooks become more and more fashioned by the mind of Jesus — the ultimate J-shaped person of history. ('Let this mind be in you that was also in Christ Jesus' — Philippians

2:5). It is not a matter of seeing a different world, but rather of seeing the same old world in a very different light and in a very different shape. Throughout Lent we shall increasingly begin to see everything in the light of the ultimate event of history — the *true* day of the Lord. It is of course the day of resurrection when he who was totally cast down was raised up to glory: when he who wore the crown of thorns and grief, is crowned in the glory of God, and when his crucifixion is seen also as his exultation at God's own right hand.

Questions for Discussion and Reflection

1. What events in my personal life have made me stop and think?

2. What events in my personal life or in our national life, have re-organized our priorities? What has fallen from the top of our list? What has been raised up to top priority from the bottom of the list?

3. 'Live this day as if 'twere thy last.' What difference would that make today?

Day of Reckoning

'Yet even now,' says the Lord, 'return to me with all your heart, with fasting, with weeping, and with mourning; and rend your hearts and not your garments.' Return to the Lord, your God, for he is gracious and merciful, slow to anger, and abounding in steadfast love, and repents of evil. Who knows whether he will not turn and repent, and leave a blessing behind him, a cereal offering and a drink offering for the Lord, your God?   Joel 2:12—14

His-story 'Who knows what can come out of all this?' Most people at the time could only see the plague of locusts and the resulting devastation and famine as unqualified 'bad news'. Yet Joel urges us to stop and look and listen. Could this not be a turning point for the people of God? For there is a greater devastation for those with eyes to see — a far more deeply rooted problem than famine or plague for those with a truly radical outlook on life. Surrounded by hostile and alien nations, Judah and Jerusalem are clearly in the firing line and are in peril of total destruction and annihilation. A day of reckoning ('the day of the Lord') is surely coming, warns Joel. It's all going to come to a head!

Yet problems are solutions in disguise. Look out! Now is the time to repent, to stop and think about it all — the plague of locusts, the international political situation, the imminent day of the Lord. In all of this what matters most is that God's people should be right with their God and that they should return to the Lord as of first priority. If they get this right, all else will follow.

Seen a different way, this could in fact be a God-given opportunity to return to God, to find all our strength and sufficiency solely in him. Then indeed God's people would be a people of the beatitudes.

The Jesus story The first beatitude on the lips of Jesus is 'Blessed are the poor in spirit, for theirs is the kingdom of heaven' (Matthew 5:3). The New English Bible translation makes that somewhat elusive phrase much clearer: 'Blessed are those who know their need of God.' It is in fact a blessed moment for a nation, for a church and for an individual when we are brought to our knees — when we ultimately know our immediate need of God. Yet what a pity that we have to wait for the last moment: that was our true position right from the start if only we had known it. So the first step in recovery for alcoholics is to acknowledge that he or she is

18

powerless (over drink). That is always the first step on the road out of the ditch. Whatever the situation may be — national catastrophe, war, disease, financial collapse, AIDS — it recalls us to our true situation as human beings — namely, our total dependency upon him upon whom all else depends. Again and again in the New Testament, Jesus recalls people to this creaturely relationship with the creator — their need to know their need of his generosity, grace and strength.

In reality, all else is delusion. That is why the rich young ruler is such a pathetic figure in the New Testament. He was not a rich young ruler at all. He was just a poor old thing! Yet the story is not so much a commentary on money, riches or his economic condition, but rather a reflection upon the human condition. The challenge to the rich young ruler is a challenge to all of us who are tempted to fill the hole in our hearts with the substitutes of money, alcohol, ambition, sexual promiscuity, etc.

So the first word on the lips of both John the Baptist and Jesus is the same as the first word on the lips of all the J-shaped prophets — 'repent'. Stop and take a second look: begin to see it all in a new light — the light of God's immense possibilities.

My story God does not send suffering to test us — that is a less than Christian view-point. Such a view is almost totally pagan in outlook. Nevertheless God can use those same sufferings (whatever they may be) in whatever way they come to us, to bring us to our senses — to make us stop and re-think it all. That time in hospital. That sudden bereavement: a sudden loss (of money, friends, family or Black Monday) — all of these can be used for good ends and by repentance we can find for ourselves the good news in the last place on earth we ever expected to find it — namely all among the bad news. Bad Friday becomes Good Friday. That which has cast us down can bring us to the point where we are ready to be raised up, but this time not in our own strength or with our own boot strings, but by the arms of a loving Saviour. He reaches down to wherever we are (for remember he has been there also) and raises us to where he is. 'Dying, and behold we live' (2 Corinthians 6:9).

So 'when these things begin to take place' do not only look out! That, by contradiction is the time to begin to 'look up' — because for J-shaped people our 'redemption is drawing nearer than when we first believed' (cp. Mark 13:28−37, Luke 21:28, Romans 13:11).

──── The Good and the Best ────

Blow the trumpet in Zion; sanctify a fast; call a solemn assembly; gather the people. Sanctify the congregation; assemble the elders; gather the children, even nursing infants. Let the bridegroom leave his room, and the bride her chamber. Between the vestibule and the altar let the priests, the ministers of the Lord, weep and say, 'Spare thy people, O Lord, and make not thy heritage a reproach, a byword among the nations. Why should they say among the peoples, "Where is their God?"'

Joel 2:15—17

His-story The cry must go out: 'Stop whatever you are doing — however important it is: even plans for marriage are overtaken by more important concerns. First things first' — that is what Joel is telling God's people. Furthermore such a radical summons is always at the heart of true repentance. At last, the 'urgent' must be overturned by the 'important' and therefore the 'ultimate'. Summon *everybody* — even children and nursing infants. Nothing can get in the way of this. Nothing is so important that it cannot be interrupted. So Joel issues a challenge. Lovemaking, marriage — all this must cease for there is now some new priority breaking into history which makes everything else fall to insignificance.

It is as though Joel has issued a 'state of emergency' — that's the true situation. So this radical prophet, in the name of God, summons the people of Israel to new priorities — first things last and last things first. This is truly radical — it strikes at the root of everything. Here is no spiritual message that would help people to feel better for a moment or two, demanding another fix at next year's renewal conference! Rather it is a challenge to a radical reappraisal of political, economic and religious priorities as the international situation becomes more clearly threatening and as the famine bites into the national economy. The message is unapologetically dramatic. It is urgent and it demands a response of action and decision from its hearers. Here is no mere proposal for discussion and debate to be put on the table, not a dialogue but rather an ultimatum which demands a change of outlook and a change of life.

The Jesus story Most of the parables of the kingdom on the lips of Jesus as we read the New Testament strike a similar note, calling for urgent decision. They are not just nice little stories with a moral to be deduced by those who like stories that have a moral conclusion. From the outset of the gospels, Jesus comes as a herald and declares unequivocally that the kingdom of God is here, now, at the root of life. It's all happening. The kingdom of God is an event not an idea. 'There is to be a wedding,' says Jesus. The invitations have gone out, and the invitations as well as courtesy demand a response: RSVP, quickly. Many begin to make excuses. They have more pressing priorities which fill their lives. So go out into the highways and hedges and find those who have nothing — nothing to lose and therefore everything to gain. They will not have a full calendar or a clash of priorities. It is the poor, those who have nothing in their diaries, their pockets or their bellies, who are the 'first' into that kingdom. They are the first to be filled with the feast prepared so generously. As Jesus tells the story, the crowd that listens begins to divide into the 'haves' and the 'have nots', the first and the last: those who've got it and those who do not even know what it is possible for them to have. The poor are the first to move forward in the crowd with eager anticipation: the rich 'are being sent empty away'. It is as though the *fulfilled* go away empty while the empty and those who know their emptiness come to the front of the crowd to reach forward to be filled with the love of Christ. The kingdom of heaven turns the claims of the kingdoms of this world literally upside down, inside out and back to front.

The story of Jesus reaches a climax. When the party is filled to overflowing it becomes obvious that it really was *the* party of the year. So there is a further turning point as the reluctant who are moving away seem to have second thoughts: 'Perhaps we might go along to the party after all, even if we go late.' Sadly, they find that it is too late to get in. The party is filled: the doors are closed.

So in the New Testament, Jesus does not invite discussion but rather he demands repentance, decision and action.

My story It is strange, ironic and even tragic how the God of creation is frequently crowded out of our lives by those very same things that he himself has created for our pleasure. Often they are good things — but they are not the best. They could never be a substitute for the one reality for which we were made — the love and worship of God. Yes, they are often good things, these substitutes, but they are not the best. The enemy of the best is not only the bad, but also the good — good, but not good enough. God longs to give us the best for he knows that in the end we will never be satisfied with anything less. The ancient collect from the *Prayer Book* turns all of this decision or discussion into a prayer of longing: it is the longing of our hearts. 'Merciful God, you have prepared for those who love you such good things as pass man's understanding. . .' The preaching of the church is intended to hold up and to hold out these 'good things' to a hungry and needy world.

─── Bonfire or Bonanza ───

Blow the trumpet in Zion; sound the alarm on my holy mountain! Let all in the inhabitants of the land tremble, for the day of the Lord is coming, it is near, a day of darkness and gloom, a day of clouds and thick darkness! Like blackness there is spread upon the mountains a great and powerful people; their like has never been from of old, nor will be again after them through the years of all generations. . . The earth quakes before them, the heavens tremble. The sun and the moon are darkened, and the stars withdraw their shining. The Lord utters his voice before his army, for his host is exceedingly great; he that executes his word is powerful. For the day of the Lord is great and very terrible; who can endure it?   Joel 2:1−2, 10−11

His-story Vanity Fair — such is the story of most history books. In 1494 Savonarola invited the inhabitants of Florence to a bonfire of vanities. So they brought out into the streets all those things (many of them harmless in themselves) which were 'vanities' and placed them on a fierce and tall bonfire. His preaching had gone to the heart of their lives and showed up their lives for the irrelevancies that they truly were: closets and closets full of vanities!

So in the teaching of Joel, there is to be a day of reckoning, the day of the Lord. There were enough false prophets around the place who encouraged the people to look forward to a future bonanza — a time when all would turn out well after all. They were not calling for a bonfire, they were promising a bonanza. Joel, like many prophets of the Old Testament, had the courage to stand out against that kind of popular message with its obvious appeal to prosperity and ease. False prophets were tempting their heroes with the affirmation summed up in such words as 'You've never had it so good!'

Yet Joel persisted that there was indeed to be a day of the Lord but that it would not be a bonanza and it would not be good news to a people whose lives were wrongly ordered with wrong priorities: for them, *au contraire*, it would be a day of 'darkness and gloom, a day of clouds and thick darkness'. The swarm of locusts had been bad enough, but that will be nothing compared with the exceedingly great 'host of God' whether that host is within history (an army from a neighbouring nation) or from outside of history — the hosts of God. In any event, the time has come to put our house in order. The message of biblical prophecy does not speak of some distant, possible disaster. It is not a projected weather forecast. It is rather an imminent warning. It interprets the signs of the times *now*. It is always a message calling for the immediate and urgent interpretation of signs — signs which are visible for all to see if only we are ready to look and listen.

The Jesus story Jesus speaks of the signs of the times in his own day. 'When you see a cloud rising in the west, you say at once, "A shower is coming"; and so it happens. And when you see the south wind blowing, you say, "There will be scorching heat"; and it happens. You hypocrites! You know how to interpret the appearance of earth and sky; but why do you not know how to interpret the present time?' (Luke 12:54–56) Why indeed? The answer is obvious. Much of our blindness is self-selective. There are none so blind as those who do not want to see. So Jesus in the New Testament speaks of the signs of the times and of what is coming on the earth. He spoke of the fall of Jerusalem which in fact occurred in AD 70, only a few years after his death on Calvary. He looked at the stones of the temple and prophesied that 'there shall not be left here one stone upon another that will not be thrown down' (Luke 21:6). He then went on to speak in Mark 13 and in the second part of Luke 21 of 'the end of everything' in language very reminiscent of the prophet Joel, and in his teaching about the day of the Lord.

My story So much of our lives are lived in Vanity Fair. There was an English prime minister in the 'fifties who coined that phrase, 'You've never had it so good!' History proved that the English were in fact just on the edge of a time when they had seldom had it quite so bad! Prosperity in itself is not wrong. Unfortunately it so often leads to a false sense of self-sufficiency and false security: that is wrong. Means become ends and important things become all-important. The day of reckoning shatters these illusions — often painfully and disastrously.

The Giver and the Gifts

'Fear not, O land; be glad and rejoice, for the Lord has done great things! Fear not, you beasts of the field, for the pastures of the wilderness are green; the tree bears its fruit, the fig tree and vine give their full yield. Be glad, O sons of Zion, and rejoice in the Lord, your God; for he has given the early rain for your vindication, he has poured down for you abundant rain, the early and the latter rain, as before. . . And it shall come to pass afterward, that I will pour out my spirit on all flesh; your sons and your daughters shall prophesy, your old men shall dream dreams, and your young men shall see visions. Even upon the men servants and maid servants in those days, I will pour out my spirit. And I will give portents in the heavens and on the earth, blood and fire and columns of smoke. The sun shall be turned to darkness, and the moon to blood, before the great and terrible day of the Lord comes.'

Joel 2:21−23, 28−31

His-story God is gift. That is the message of the scriptures from cover to cover. All life is gift. There is no such person as a self-made man. Joel recalls the people of God to learn to live as the children of God. He will *give* 'the early and the latter rain'. But notice, those rains are a gift. Then those very areas ravaged by plague and drought will become fruitful and green. For Joel is at pains to teach that all life corporately and individually is a gift, and certainly that new life — the life of springtime — is quite obviously and clearly a gift. The winter of discontent can only be replaced by the fruitful and generous gift of spring. To know that is to discover the very heart of true renewal.

Yet the greatest gift of all that God longs to give us — as with all lovers — is the gift of himself: the gift of his very own Spirit. It is often the most unlikely and the least qualified people who receive that Gift. The talented, the rich, the young, successful and the beautiful are the most tempted to live as though life is what you make it for yourself. They are the last, however, into the kingdom — the new order of things. They are the very last to receive God's many and generous gifts. They come with their pockets, bellies and diaries all filled, filled so full that there is no space left for God to fill in their lives. So in the Old Testament it is the barren who are given the gift of children and in the New Testament the point is made even more clearly — the Virgin is with child of the Holy Spirit.

So again and again in history the prophets speak of a time of preparation (rather like Lent) when we are stripped of our pretensions and substitute goods. Such times are times of darkness when the 'sun has turned to darkness' so that the most reliable things are then seen to have the capacity to fail and disappoint us. We must not place our ultimate trust in any*thing*, only in some*body* — the living God. Our ultimate concern is not even in the rising sun, important and dependable though it is, for there is One even mightier and he is gracious and generous — and he has risen most assuredly with 'healing in his wings' (Malachi 4:2).

The Jesus story In the New Testament, Jesus teaches his disciples to live as children of a loving and generous father. In the kingdom of God there is no need to 'lay up treasure' and to hoard. We need not care so much about what we have saved but rather whether we ourselves *are* saved. And in all of this, we can be released ultimately from any anxiety — for even daily bread will be *given*. So we are invited by Jesus to consider and give our minds not *primarily* to the stock exchange but rather to 'the lilies of the field' and to observe how they grow and multiply. 'They neither toil nor spin,' Jesus reminds us, 'yet even Solomon in all his glory was not arrayed like one of these' (Matthew 6:28−29). For remember, that if we who like to speak of ourselves as 'self-made' men and women 'know how to give good gifts' to our children, then how much more will our 'Father, who is in heaven, give good things' and indeed the greatest gift of all — the Holy Spirit — 'to those who ask him' (cp. Matthew 7:11 and Luke 11:13)? Little wonder St Peter sees the *gift* of the Spirit at Pentecost as the true fulfilment of this passage from Joel.

My story It is when we are finished that God can begin — when we are empty that he can fill us with his Spirit and his love. It is often the darkest period before the dawn and it is so often when we are having our break *down* that God can at last break *through*. That is our 'day of the Lord'. That is our day of reckoning, reversal and contradiction. It is at the very roots of true resurrection and renewal; we experience this sign of contradiction at the heart of life and history. Hence Christians practise fasting as a sacramental and bodily sign of self-emptying, but always in anticipation of that true fulfilment by the filling of the Holy Spirit through our Pentecost prayer. For that also — prayer — is always a gift and certainly must not be mistaken for a skill, a technique or a talent. St Paul reminds us, 'It is not you who pray' but rather the Holy Spirit who prays in and through us as we are caught up in the 'givingness' of love between the Father and the Son.

JACOB: THE MANIPULATOR

JACOB is the one of the darkest and possibly one of the least attractive of God's J-shaped people in the Old Testament. His very name means by derivation the one who 'over-reaches', 'supplants' and 'beguiles'. Yet in every way, Jacob is a sign of contradiction. Jacob is pictured in the Old Testament as one who relies on his natural strength and cunning and guile. Yet in the hands of God he becomes, after wrestling with God, 'Israel' which means — also by derivation — 'May God show *his* strength' (Jerusalem Bible). He was chosen by God as an instrument of God's strength and supplanted Esau, his brother, who was in fact the first-born son of Isaac. We know from the story in the Old Testament of how Jacob robbed Esau of his birthright. Esau was very much his father's boy, while Jacob was his mother's son. He dwelt in the darkness and the shadows of the tent, we are told, while Esau delighted in hunting, the outdoor life of the athlete, demonstrating physical strength.

It is through Jacob that the promises of God which were first made to Abraham are handed down. For Esau, life is straightforward: for Jacob, it is subtle, dark and resembles a labyrinth of surprises. So we should not be surprised that in fact it was Jacob who inherited the promises of God. He is reckoned righteous by a second birth and even a new and second name. He clearly has no qualifications to be chosen except the qualification of that first beatitude, 'How blest are those who know their need of God' (Matthew 5:3 NEB).

For in wrestling with God, Jacob was broken, lamed and his life was re-ordered. Through worship he finds God in his life at the most unlikely place of all — in the place of his fear and darkness. Finally, in the ultimate reconciliation with his brother Esau, he realizes that he (Jacob) is the object of Esau's favour — a favour which cannot be bought. At that very moment he declares that he has seen the face of God in the face of Esau, his despised brother.

Somewhat rejected by his earthly father, Jacob discovers what the psalmist expresses so beautifully — 'When my father and mother forsake me; the Lord taketh me up' (Psalm 27). Yet the Lord's favour cannot be won by talent. It cannot be bought or manipulated. Jacob strives to manipulate life and relationships in his favour. In his wrestling with God, however, he finds that in the end it is God who manipulates him and re-shapes him to be a vessel of his grace and a bearer of his word.

Jacob is not only re-named (Israel) but he is re-shaped in the firm and loving hands of God to a righteousness not of his own devising or contriving. Weak in the arm but strong in the head (the opposite of Esau) he was initially a recipe for disaster — until he met God and was re-shaped into the J-shape of God's devising.

Jacob is a kind of reluctant witness to the grace of God at work in the most unpromising lives and as such he stands in that long line of those who have been chosen, not for what they are as self-made, self-sufficient men and women; but rather for what, by God's grace, they can be made in the firm and manipulating hands of God's love. It is God's hands which re-fashion our lives. We do not need to pull strings, but rather allow him to tug at our heels (as Jacob tugged at Esau's heel in his mother's womb). Lovingly but surely God can then set our feet in a new direction and on a new road.

By contradiction and strange inversion, it was Jacob who glorified God more than Esau his brother, for he witnessed to the light of God's glory even in the shadows and in the darkness of much of his life.

How odd of God to choose the Jews!

How odd of God to choose Jacob rather than Esau!

How even 'odder' of God to choose folks like you and me to be the vessels of his grace and the vehicles of his glory!

Questions for Discussion and Reflection

1. What are my strengths? What are my weaknesses? In what ways do I need saving from both?

2. In what ways are worship and conversion related?

3. In what ways does insecurity hinder maturity?

Back to Front

Abraham was the father of Isaac, and Isaac was forty years old when he took to wife Rebekah, the daughter of Bethuel the Aramean of Paddan-aram, the sister of Laban the Aramean. And Isaac prayed to the Lord for his wife, because she was barren; and the Lord granted his prayer, and Rebekah his wife conceived. The children struggled together within her; and she said, 'If it is thus, why do I live?' So she went to inquire of the Lord. And the Lord said to her,

'Two nations are in your womb,
and two peoples, born of you, shall be divided;
the one shall be stronger than the other,
the elder shall serve the younger.'   Genesis 25:19—23

His-story   Again and again throughout the Old Testament the Jews delighted to tell the story of their heredity and their family tree in terms of motherhood as a gift from God. It started with Sarah who was barren and well past the age of childbearing. Nevertheless the angel promises her a son. She is so amused by the obvious absurdity of the angel's message that she bursts into peals of laughter. The son is born. He is appropriately called 'a joke (Isaac)'. Yes, God, you really must be joking! And so the theme of barren women becoming fruitful mothers occurs again and again throughout the Old Testament.

Hannah is barren yet she is *given* Samuel as a son whom she in turn gives back to the Lord as surely as Abraham was prepared to sacrifice Isaac upon the altar of God's greater love for the boy. Hannah sings the J-shaped song, that song of *revolution* rather than straightforward *evolution*. 'My heart exults in the Lord. My strength is exalted in the Lord. . . because I rejoice in thy salvation. . . The bows of the mighty are broken, but the feeble gird on strength. Those who are full have hired themselves out for bread, but those who are hungry have ceased to hunger. The barren has born seven, but she who has many children is forlorn. . . The Lord makes poor and makes rich; he brings low, he also exalts. He raises up the poor from the dust; he lifts the needy from the ash heap, to make them sit with princes and inherit a seat of honour' (1 Samuel 2:1—8).

This theme of a topsy-turvy world of contradiction (this J-shaped kingdom) is a constant theme in the Old Testament and reaches its climax and fullest orchestration with Mary (the virgin who is with child) in the recast version of Hannah's original song — the song we call 'The Magnificat'

(Luke 1:46–55). Mary is the last (and therefore of course the first!) of a long line of those who bear the new life. That new life is always seen as a direct gift from God. The New Testament begins like the Old with an angel talking to a very unlikely woman about the birth of a son! It is a huge joke from cover to cover! Jesus is the new Isaac in more ways than one. So Jacob takes his place in this long line of contradictions and as the last-born, becomes the first-born and the inheritor of the promised kingdom.

The Jesus story Jesus takes up this theme. He teaches again and again in the New Testament about his father's kingdom in which the first are last and the last are first. He wants us to see everything in a new light. Our identity as his people relates us to all those other signs of contradiction who have gone before us. Jacob is an important chapter in that long story. Mary in the New Testament fulfils all that theme of motherhood by promise which is there for us between the lines in the Old Testament. In other words, Mary shows us supremely in the New Testament the pattern and shape of our redemption which we can faintly discern in the pages of the Old. She sings loud and clearly and with even more confidence the song of Hannah.

'He has put down the mighty from their thrones,
and exalted those of low degree;
he has filled the hungry with good things,
and the rich he has sent empty away.'
(Luke 1:52–53)

My story What does all this say about the way our world reveres success, strength and power? We need the love of God to turn all this world-view of ours head over heels — really in love. Only then can we become vehicles and vessels which receive life as a gift from God — a gift which always points to him and to his glory. St Paul discovered that it is in our weakness that we are given strength; it is in our defeat that we are raised up and when we are willing to be last (the elder serving the younger), God makes us first. To God be the glory!

── Projection or Reflection ──

When her days to be delivered were fulfilled, behold, there were twins in her womb. The first came forth red, all his body like a hairy mantle; so they called his name Esau. Afterward his brother came forth, and his hand had taken hold of Esau's heel; so his name was called Jacob. Isaac was sixty years old when she bore them.

When the sons grew up, Esau was a skilful hunter, a man of the field, while Jacob was a quiet man, dwelling in tents. Isaac loved Esau, because he ate of his game; but Rebekah loved Jacob.

Genesis 25:24—28

His-story Jacob was clearly not much earthly use! Esau was the skilful one — the extrovert, the hunter and the more practical of the twins. He was the man of energy and action; Jacob was the man of reflection (not projection), smooth (literally) and calculating. Yet here again we have to learn that God's ways are not our ways, for God does not look on the outward appearance, but upon the heart. We are reminded in the choice of David for king that 'the Lord sees not as man sees' (1 Samuel 16:7). So when choosing David as the anointed one in the Old Testament, the prophet Samuel is reminded not to have regard for 'appearance' or for 'the height of his stature'. That is not the grounds on which God chooses his servants.

Esau could easily impress his earthly father by his achievements and especially by his 'manly ways and appearance'. His hairy body and his expertise in the field where he was a skilful hunter all cut an impressive appearance. On the other hand, Jacob was more the introvert. The thoughtful reflective person — something perhaps of a mother's boy (v. 28). Of the two it is not immediately obvious why God should choose Jacob as the one through whom the J-shaped promises made earlier to Abraham should be inherited. Which profile is more striking from God's point of view?

The Jesus story In the New Testament Paul is supremely the surprise packet in the apostolic band. Yet here again it is important to get hold of the right end of the stick. Paul was not an impressive personality as he is so often caricatured in contemporary accounts of his life. In fact he warns the Corinthian church that although they are God's chosen people — the new Israel (Jacob's men and women) — in fact not many of them were wealthy or clever by the world's standards. For that must not be the yardstick by which we measure things in the kingdom. 'Not that we are competent of ourselves,' he tells the church in Corinth, 'to claim anything as coming from us; our competence is from God' (2 Corinthians 3:5). Eusebius (c. 262—340), the father of church history, tells us that tradition had always insisted that St Paul was not physically attractive or particularly impressive. The general opinion in the days of Eusebius (and almost certainly such a tradition was handed down) insisted that Paul had been a little man with bandy legs, a red nose and that furthermore he was someone who could not speak very well. Just the sort of person God seems to choose!

My story It is often the handicapped who teach us most about our skills which we are always in danger of taking for granted. It was the deaf Beethoven who taught us most about how to listen and whose themes and melodies strike the ear most powerfully. In fact, we are not asked to be either sentimental or unrealistic about handicaps of any kind in ourselves or others. But we should nevertheless remember and recall what God has been able to do by his strength *through* those handicaps and through our weakness; by his wisdom through our foolishness. We certainly need to be capable of second thoughts about all our selection and election processes — in matters great and small. In our world it is nearly always Esau who would get all the awards and the trophies! Perhaps we all need to rewrite our profiles for any search committee or any selection process if we are really to make an impression in the kingdom of God rather than in the kingdom of this world. We need men and women who *re*flect rather than *pro*ject.

Who Cares?

Once when Jacob was boiling pottage, Esau came in from the field, and he was famished. And Esau said to Jacob, 'Let me eat some of that red pottage, for I am famished!' (Therefore his name was called Edom.) Jacob said, 'First sell me your birthright.' Esau said, 'I am about to die; of what use is a birthright to me?' Jacob said, 'Swear to me first.' So he swore to him, and sold his birthright to Jacob. Then Jacob gave Esau bread and pottage of lentils, and he ate and drank, and rose and went his way. Thus Esau despised his birthright.   Genesis 25:29−34

His-story The privileged all too easily take for granted their gifts and fail to cherish what they have always thought of as theirs 'by right'. Equally, the 'underprivileged' are tempted to covet, grasp and steal in less than honourable ways and to contest for their 'rights'. So in the story of Esau and Jacob, Esau took his birthright for granted: Jacob acquired it by grasping for it and took Esau's birthright away.

For as the elder of the two (by only just a few minutes) Esau held the birthright by right. He was the privileged child from birth. Yet he did not cherish that gift, the story tells us. He took it for granted. So he ended up selling it for a mess of pottage. On the other hand and at the same time (again in only a few minutes) the grasping manipulation of Jacob was quick to take advantage. He steals what is not his both in this story and in the other longer account when Jacob, encouraged by his mother, pretends to be Esau by bringing his father game to eat. In return his blind old father gives to Jacob the blessing which, by right, belonged only to the elder son and the first-born — Esau.

Strangely enough, however, *by approach*, Jacob is nearer the heart of the matter than Esau. Esau took his birthright for granted and priced it too low. Jacob grasped for it and priced it too highly. (He was dishonest and cunning.) Nevertheless in the eternal scheme of things, Jacob knew what he wanted and was prepared to move heaven and earth to get it. What he did was not right, but because he wanted something badly enough he was the kind of man who would one day stumble into the edges of something which was real treasure. Esau did not treasure his birthright enough; Jacob treasured it too much. Jacob however in the end was more likely to go out of his way to achieve that treasure because he was disturbed and not complacent; he was passionate and not apathetic or indifferent.

The Jesus story The heroes in the New Testament stories of the kingdom of heaven are more like Jacob than Esau. Take for example the parable of the treasure hidden in the field; or on the other hand, the woman searching for the coin. The heroes in those stories are prepared to move heaven and earth to get what they want. Furthermore there is that difficult parable of the unjust steward. In all of these stories, the people who are commended are people who are ready to go to the ends of the earth and to stop at nothing to get what they really want. In that account of the unjust steward, as with Jacob, the story is not a very moralistic one. The heroes are not being commended for what they did but for their attitudes, their passion and their single-mindedness. They knew what they wanted (albeit the wrong things) and they were ready to go to any lengths to get them. There is always more hope for people who care too much than for those who do not care enough. Whatever else God's J-shaped people may be, they are essentially passionate and not apathetic.

My story Most of us most of the time are too easily pleased. 'It would seem that our Lord finds our desires not too strong, but too weak. We are half-hearted creatures, fooling about with drink and sex and ambition when infinite joy is offered us, like an ignorant child who wants to go on making mud-pies in a slum because he cannot imagine what is meant by the offer of a holiday at the sea. We are far too easily pleased' (C.S. Lewis, *The Weight of Glory*).

In a strange way, Jacob was on the right road going in the wrong direction. As he was to discover, God had prepared for him another birthright which surpassed even his wildest dreams and envy! God had prepared for Jacob a real treasure for which it was indeed worth going to the ends of the world in order to acquire. Yet what Jacob had to learn, we all need to learn: the real treasure can only be received as a free gift — that second birth, the gift of eternal life. We do not get it by grasping for it; but rather by allowing it to grasp hold of us.

——— Security or Maturity? ———

And (Jacob) came to a certain place, and stayed there that night, because the sun had set. Taking one of the stones of the place, he put it under his head and lay down in that place to sleep. And he dreamed that there was a ladder set up on the earth, and the top of it reached to heaven; and behold, the angels of God were ascending and descending on it! And behold, the Lord stood above it and said, 'I am the Lord, the God of Abraham your father and the God of Isaac; the land on which you lie I will give to you and to your descendants; and your descendants shall be like the dust of the earth, and you shall spread abroad to the west and to the east and to the north and to the south; and by you and your descendants shall all the families of the earth bless themselves. Behold, I am with you and will keep you wherever you go, and will bring you back to this land; for I will not leave you until I have done that of which I have spoken to you.' Then Jacob awoke from his sleep and said, 'Surely the Lord is in this place; and I did not know it.' And he was afraid, and said, 'How awesome is this place! This is none other than the house of God, and this is the gate of heaven.'

Genesis 28:11—17

His-story The theme of nomadic pilgrimage which is set at the heart of the whole record and story of God's chosen people is taken up here again (as with Abraham at the outset). Esau of course is more content to stay at home: Jacob is restless, afraid of Esau and clearly has not found either a wife, nor indeed has he found himself. He needs to set out in order to find himself.

So he leaves Beersheba and he goes to Haran. In one sense he is running away. In another he needs to lose himself and lose his way in order to find his true self and to find God's way. In any event, to cling to security, home and family will mean that he will never find maturity, heaven and God. It is our implanted yearning for heaven, as mysterious as homing pigeons, which makes all of us restless. Yet in one sense we can never go back home — that would disappoint us eternally. The warmth and draw of home and family points in another direction — it points to our ultimate home which is nothing less than heaven itself.

Yet Jacob, thinking he has left behind the best, lies down to sleep with stones for a pillow (perhaps home would have been better after all for a good night's sleep?). In that less-than-comfortable position he is deeply disturbed and God is able to speak to him in a dream. Often God can do more for his people in sleep because we do not get in the way so much. 'Surely the Lord is in all of this' — this place — this family row and all that had led him to leave home. 'This is none other than the house of God, and this is the gate of heaven,' exclaimed Jacob as he comes to the first turning point in his life. Notice the first turning point occurs when he is no longer in control. In fact he is asleep — at least now God can take over and begin to manage things! So it is in worship that Jacob loses himself and finally discovers self-transcendance — the only key with which a personality can unlock the door to true liberation and ultimate freedom.

The Jesus story In the New Testament we see Jesus teaching as he travels and the disciples learning as they walk on pilgrimage.

If men and women are to follow in that pilgrimage once again they will become signs of contradiction and will need to identify with all those other J-shaped people, like Jacob, who lost themselves in order to find their true selves in the self-transcendence of worship. Christians are displaced people. They are pilgrims all the way from baptism to heaven. We must beware of making our homes on earth too permanent or too comfortable — they are not intended to be built to last! We were made for tents on earth, with pegs that yield to the wind of the Spirit.

My story There is a rhythm in our growth towards maturity. G.K. Chesterton reminds us there is a time when the road points to the pub, but another time when the pub points back to the road! There is a time to rest our head and put our feet up. There is another time to be on our feet and doing — on the move. 'In my Father's house,' says Jesus, 'are many resting places' (John 14:2). The Authorised Version's translation is misleading here. They are not 'mansions' — to say the least that is an unfortunate mis-translation. For it is at just this point that so many of us go so wrong. We would like of course to be promised permanent mansions, comfortable dead-ends. On the contrary, even the best of pillows would feel like stones compared with the ultimate rest and warmth of heaven. So in the meantime (provisionally) we must settle for 'motels' conveniently located for a night's sleep, for rest, for restoration and renewal. Yet we must always be ready to get back on the road the moment the sun has risen. Wrong security now could rob us of ultimate maturity later.

—— The Well of Life ——

Then Laban said to Jacob, 'Because you are my kinsman, should you therefore serve me for nothing? Tell me, what shall your wages be?' Now Laban had two daughters; the name of the older was Leah, and the name of the younger was Rachel. Leah's eyes were weak, but Rachel was beautiful and lovely. Jacob loved Rachel; and he said, 'I will serve you seven years for your younger daughter Rachel.' Laban said, 'It is better that I give her to you than that I should give her to any other man; stay with me.' So Jacob served seven years for Rachel, and they seemed to him but a few days because of the love he had for her.

Genesis 29:15—20

His-story At last Jacob finds Uncle Laban's house. He goes to the well at the watering place in a nearby village. The well in the Eastern world is the place of meeting which all families and travellers need to frequent. It is a great leveller. It is the centre of communication and community and of course the place where all the gossips gather also. In the ancient world if you wanted to find out anything about anybody then you would spend time loitering by the well for long enough and you would soon hear all about it.

So it is from the well that Jacob is led first to Uncle Laban and his kinsfolk and from there to the woman he was to love and to marry — Rachel. Furthermore it was through Rachel, at first barren, that God continued the line of his chosen people — the family of God — with the birth of Joseph in her later life.

Yet life in Laban's house was not happy for Jacob. There was cheating, suspicion and revenge. It was not long before Rachel and Jacob found themselves back out on the road — back home to old Isaac in Canaan.

The Jesus story The family of God (through water and baptism) cuts across all other family and national loyalties. For the Jew, the family was the basic building block — and so it should be. But it must not stop there. We must not idolize our blood families. Blood is thicker than water, but water and the spirit together are thicker and richer than blood. Jesus has some hard words to say about family life if it becomes an end in itself. Family loyalties point beyond themselves, or should do, to the larger loyalties of the family of the kingdom. 'Truly, I say to you, there is no one who has left house or brothers or sisters or mother or father or children or lands, for my sake and for the gospel, who will not receive a hundredfold now in this time, houses and brothers and sisters and mothers and children and lands, with persecutions, and in the age to come eternal life. But many that are first shall be last, and the last first' (Mark 10:29–31). In other words our blood loyalties need to be re-ordered through the waters of baptism and at the well of life. It is in that sense that Jesus tells us to 'hate' father and mother. On another occasion, when the mother and brothers of Jesus are waiting for him outside he asks the apparently hard question, ' "Who are my mother and my brothers?" And looking around on those who sat about him, he said, "Here are my mother and my brothers! Whoever does the will of God is my brother, and sister, and mother" ' (Mark 3:33–35).

It was by the Samaritan well that Jesus talked to the woman of the reordering of the nations in which all would enter into the true worship of the Father 'neither on this mountain nor in Jerusalem' (John 4:21). One of the last words on the lips of Jesus from the cross re-orders human bonds of friendship and family: 'When Jesus saw his mother, and the disciple whom he loved standing near, he said to his mother, "Woman behold your son!" Then he said to the disciple, "Behold, your mother!" And from that hour the disciple took her to his own home' (John 19:26–27). By baptism in water and the Spirit, we are introduced to that wider loyalty — the family of God stretching back to Jacob and to Rachel and to Abraham — and all this through Jesus on his mother's side, as it were!

My story 'The family that prays together stays together', we are told. Yes, and so it does. Yet that is the first step and only the first step in loyalty. If it stops there it does not go far enough. The saying perhaps should read (both for our families and also for nations): 'The family that prays together stays together; the family that stays together, decays together!' For the family is not an end in itself. It is an essential and important building block on the way to the larger edifice of the worldwide family of the church and ultimately to that eternal family of the kingdom of God. In that family we are all baptized into one body — Jews or Greeks, slaves or free — for 'all were made to drink of one Spirit' at the true well of real life — eternal life (1 Corinthians 12:13).

The Turning Point

And Jacob was left alone; and a man wrestled with him until the breaking of the day. When the man saw that he did not prevail against Jacob, he touched the hollow of his thigh; and Jacob's thigh was put out of joint as he wrestled with him. Then he said, 'Let me go, for the day is breaking.' But Jacob said, 'I will not let you go, unless you bless me.' And he said to him, 'What is your name?' And he said, 'Jacob'. Then he said, 'Your name shall no more be called Jacob, but Israel, for you have striven with God and with men, and have prevailed.' Then Jacob asked him, 'Tell me, I pray, your name.' But he said, 'Why is it that you ask my name?' And there he blessed him. So Jacob called the name of the place Peniel, saying, 'For I have seen God face to face, and yet my life is preserved.' The sun rose upon him as he passed Penuel, limping because of his thigh.   Genesis 32:24—31

His-story Jacob the manipulator is finally out-manipulated by God. The story tells us that at last Jacob is alone: his defences are down and it is night. At last he is face to face after years of fleeing and running away from it all. Now there is no way round it, out of it or over it. Now at last he must face up to it. So we find him wrestling with God. He pits his strength against the strength of God. He prevails and yet he is broken by it — his thigh was put out of joint, we are told, as the dawn was breaking. We can picture him limping across the desert.

What an incredible story! Yet at last Jacob's strengths were re-ordered — thank God. Now he is God's man. For not only do we need redeeming from our weaknesses, failures and sins but essentially we also need to be saved from our strengths. Jacob had always been in control — the manipulator who overreached, as he did in his mother's womb. Indeed his name from birth had indicated such a personality. Now at last he who had always overreached was finally overtaken and God took over his life. As the sun was rising at last it began to dawn upon Jacob where his real strength was to be found. At last he was under new management. What might have been the end of everything (surely to see God face to face would be to die according to the teaching of the old Israel) turned out after all to be the new beginning of a truly God-centred life. Called, chosen — at last, he was converted. He was turned around, but all this was not without pain, discomfort and a profound disturbance at the centre of his whole being. Now he was to be a new man with a new name, a new identity and 'a new song to sing' (St Augustine).

The Jesus story The desert in the Bible is the place of realism, where the light and the darkness, the heat and the cold, the day and the night are merciless and know no deceptions. You cannot cheat the reality of the desert.

So Jesus identifies with many of the J-shaped people of the Old Testament by himself going to the desert immediately after his baptism. What appears however to be the most God-forsaken place on earth turns out after all to be the place of wrestling with reality. But Jesus, unlike Jacob, seeks to do God's will and is not fleeing from God. So inevitably he wrestles not with God but with the devil. In both cases, Jesus and Jacob, it is a power struggle. Yet it is in the desert that we discover where real power is to be found: not from the devil — he seeks to seduce Jesus with the promise of worldly power. Jesus rejects that power at the beginning of his ministry (at the hands of the devil) and again at the end of his ministry (on the lips of Pilate). Real power and real strength are from God alone, given to us in our weakness. In the desert Jesus discerned his true vocation and learned to rely on the sources of his real strength and the nature of that true power which comes from God alone and is given freely to us in our weakness.

My story 'In the desert of the heart, let the springs of healing start' (W.H. Auden). Where is the most obviously Godforsaken place in the geography of my life? It is there that I need to go alone to find 'the God of my strength and my salvation'. For it will not necessarily be my weaknesses and sins that will keep me out of heaven — but perhaps my strengths and my talents. It is my strengths and my talents for which I must thank God so that — as with the eucharistic bread — he may break and re-order them in such a way as to turn my life around. In my conversion there will be inevitable pain which will become the pearl. My weaknesses will become my strengths and my assumed strengths can be surrendered — at last setting me free from the need to win. In that moment, I shall know who I am, and whose I am; the name that God alone can give me — God's nickname for me as surely as Israel was God's nickname for Jacob.

Impressive or Expressive?

But Esau ran to meet (Jacob), and embraced him, and fell on his neck and kissed him, and they wept. And when Esau raised his eyes and saw the women and children, he said, 'Who are these with you?' Jacob said, 'The children whom God has graciously given your servant'. . . . Esau said, 'What do you mean by all this company which I met?' Jacob answered, 'To find favour in the sight of my lord.' But Esau said, 'I have enough, my brother; keep what you have for yourself.' Jacob said, 'No, I pray you, if I have found favour in your sight, then accept my present from my hand; for truly to see your face is like seeing the face of God, with such favour have you received me. Accept, I pray you, my gift that is brought to you, because God has dealt graciously with me, and because I have enough.' Thus he urged him, and he took it.

Genesis 33:4−5, 8−11

His-story It was the last thing in the world Jacob could ever have expected! Here was Esau, whom he had not seen for years and from whom he had fled for his life, coming up to Jacob and actually embracing him. 'He fell on his neck and kissed him.' This is the stuff of which reconciliation is truly made. Yet what a surprise — this is indeed a turn-up for the book.

It is of course the very opposite of what we might expect. After all, Jacob and Esau were old enemies. Jacob is a very different man from the man who stole his brother's birthright and cheated Isaac, his old father. When Esau asks about the women and children, Jacob speaks of them now only as gracious gifts from God. Yet still he is trying to win favour with Esau and to impress his elder brother — or is he? Esau makes it quite clear that he does not need any presents — 'I have enough, my brother,' he replied. His reply, however, is utterly gracious. Then Jacob further retorts in words that finally give away the real score: 'Truly to see your face is like seeing the face of God,' he tells his brother, 'with such favour have you received me. Accept, I pray you, my gift.' This is not any longer the old Jacob trying to impress, manipulate, or be in control. This is the new Israel, 'ransomed, healed, restored, forgiven'. Jacob truly wishes to express his debt of deep gratitude for his brother's God-like, gracious and loving forgiveness.

The Jesus story At the heart of the Jesus story is the greatest contradiction of all. 'Love your enemies; and pray for those who persecute you, so that you may be sons of your Father who is in heaven' (Matthew 5:44–45). For we are sons of the same Father and therefore we are brothers.

Brothers then — not competitors, as it was at the first birth. Now, born again, we are named by God for his loving purposes of reconciliation. In our turn, we extend to others the forgiveness we have so generously and graciously received from our Father in heaven. It's hard to know quite where you are in the teaching of Jesus — it is so very J-shaped! It is hard to know who are our enemies and who are our friends.

My story And so we must identify with those other J-shaped people who have learned the strange profile and contours of the heavenly country. Surely the story of the prodigal son is deliberately J-shaped in identifying with the story of the reconciliation of Jacob and Esau. Even the words in which Jesus casts these events are significant: 'While he (the prodigal son) was yet at a distance, his father saw him and had compassion, and ran and embraced and kissed him' (Luke 15:20). That is what I must do if I wish to take my place in that long line of people who have given up trying to *impress* because they are so busy trying to *express* their love and gratitude for total forgiveness so graciously and generously given. That experience literally turns my whole world upside down and head over heels.

So the family of Isaac is healed and reconciled. Alienation always manifests itself in dis-ease of some kind. Since birth there had been alienation and competition between Jacob and Esau. At last they are reconciled.

Often it is those who are closest to us who test us most in the matter of reconciliation and forgiveness. They mirror back to us uncomfortable likenesses, not least if we are twins. The closer we are to someone the more difficult we find it to be reconciled with what is of us, in them. Family rifts are the most costly to heal. Charity begins at home.

JOSHUA: THE VICTOR

KNOWN originally as Hoshea which means 'salvation' (see Numbers 13:8, 16; Deuteronomy 32:44), his name was changed by Moses to Joshua which means significantly 'Jehovah is salvation'. Moses had changed his name after Hoshea, his newly appointed commander, had put down the Amalekites in the early months of the Exodus story.

Joshua is at root the same as the name for Jesus. Yet Joshua needed to learn, as did Peter and Paul — the commanders-in-chief of the 'army' of Jesus Christ — that God's strength is made perfect in our weakness. That was a hard lesson for a young 'successful' warrior. When he was sent with others by Moses to spy out the land of Canaan, the report came back that the inhabitants of the land of Canaan were so big and powerful that the spies felt like grasshoppers in comparison! Not unnaturally, the news terrified the people of Israel who were all ready to return and flee back to Egypt. It was Joshua (newly named) who stood up to refute this defeatism. The strength of Israel, he contended, did not lie in their size, their numbers or their *own* strength, but rather in their obedience to Jehovah — the God of battles. His advice was so unpopular, as it turned out, that the people threatened to stone him.

Then, in a vision from God, the Lord assures the people of Israel of the gift of the land of promise if they in their turn will be faithful and obedient to Jehovah. They must learn that therein is their true strength — for, 'I will make of you', promises Jehovah, 'a nation greater and mightier than they'.

So it is that Joshua emerges as the J-shaped victor and warrior of Israel.

After the death of Moses, Joshua, as the oldest man in Israel (well into his nineties) leads the people of Israel through the Jordan, through the walls of Jericho and through mighty battles to the point where they do indeed inherit the land of Canaan — that land 'flowing with milk and honey'.

'To frail earthen vessels and things of no worth,' God entrusts his riches. The saints in every age have turned our value systems on their heads. So Mary, the most fruitful virgin of Israel, that supremely J-shaped person, sings now the fully orchestrated version of the song of revolution:

'My soul magnifies the Lord,
and my spirit rejoices in God my Saviour. . .

for he who is mighty has done great things for me.' It is to the old, the outcasts, the despised and the 'useless' that God entrusts his greatest gifts. Joshua by his very name was rescued from the great human delusion — namely, that we are saved by our own strength, by our own worldly wisdom, by our personality or by striving to be impressive. The saints are not busy trying to *impress* others because they are too busy trying to *express* the love of God which they have discovered for themselves. It is often said of God's J-shaped people, as it was said with derision of Jesus: 'He saved others, himself he cannot save'.

Joshua, God's great warrior of the Old Testament, was made perfect in weakness and so emerged as the man of real power in his old age. The victories are clearly seen as God's victories, in just the same way as the supreme victory of history on Calvary Hill was won by God in Christ. '*Christus Victor*' is one of several interpretations of what Jesus achieved on the cross. He took on the devil and the forces of evil, and triumphed.

So Jesus is the true victor and embodies in himself all the J-shaped people before and after him. Jesus, together with the saints, manifests quite clearly that supreme contradiction in history — namely, that it is in defeat that we are made victorious, in weakness *given* strength, and therefore, eventually and ultimately, in death that we are raised up to new life.

Questions for Discussion and Reflection

1.   In what ways may I need to be disloyal to the kingdoms of this world in order to be loyal to the Kingdom of God?

2.   In what ways do Christians 'live for others'?

3.   Where do we see evidence for the assumption that evil is more than simply the absence of good?

┌─────────── **Information and Inspiration** ───────────┐

After the death of Moses the servant of the Lord, the Lord said to Joshua the son on Nun, Moses' minister, 'Moses my servant is dead; now therefore arise, go over this Jordan, you and all this people, into the land which I am giving to them, to the people of Israel. Every place that the sole of your foot will tread upon I have given to you, as I promised to Moses. . . Be strong and of good courage; be not frightened, neither be dismayed; for the Lord your God is with you wherever you go.'

Then Joshua commanded the officers of the people, 'Pass through the camp, and command the people, "Prepare your provisions; for within three days you are to pass over this Jordan, to go in to take possession of the land which the Lord your God gives you to possess".'

Joshua 1:1−3, 9−11

└──┘

His-story It takes two very different people: one kind to lead a revolution, but quite another to establish a kingdom. Moses brought the people of God out of Egypt and led them through the desert. Such a hazardous passage required both a leader and an educator (from '*educo*', to draw out the capacity and potential locked and imprisoned within). So it is that in the Old Testament Moses is the great lawgiver: he literally educates the people of Israel at the same time as drawing them out and leading them out from the bondage of Egypt. True education draws out what is locked within and liberates us.

Joshua is rather different. His vocation is to establish a kingdom and it is not for nothing that his name is identified at root with Jesus who came to establish the kingdom of God in our hearts. So as we have seen, Joshua means 'salvation' — and that is much more than education. Joshua is a salvation figure — a key figure in salvation history. He will perfect and complete what was promised to Moses.

Yet as we have seen, Joshua was an older man who, by God's grace alone, was enabled to make a fresh start — a new beginning. So we see that all the imagery is the imagery of new birth, life through death, and life laid down in the crossing over of water. For new life always begins the other side of water — Joshua, Jordan and Jesus are all closely identified with that new life the other side of the waters of 'baptism'.

The Jesus story Jesus began to preach about the kingdom when he came up out of the Jordan, after his baptism. After he was 'baptised by John in the Jordan' he came into Israel 'preaching the gospel of God, and saying, "The time is fulfilled, and the kingdom of God is at hand"' (Mark 1:9, 14–15). In Jesus we have, however, both the new Moses and the new Joshua combined. Jesus delivers us from the bondage of sin, he leads us through the wilderness of sin and teaches us about the new law of grace and the new kingdom of God. But he goes further than mere education. Education and information are never enough in themselves. Jesus breaks through the walls and barriers of sin and alienation and takes us into that kingdom of his love and salvation. He is supremely the witness in history to God's power to save. He is literally the God of battles. The victory is his and it is assured.

My story The world needs salvation not just education. Education is never enough in itself. For the test of the Christian faith is not so much whether it makes good men and women better but whether it has the power to make bad men and women holy. We need Joshua as well as Moses to tell the full story of Exodus. The task of the church is to demolish the fortress of evil with the greatest force and strength of all — the love and grace of God made known to us in Jesus Christ our Saviour. Although victory is assured, the battle still rages, however, and God's J-shaped people are called in each generation to serve in the ranks.

Jesus is of course an example of godly life, a teacher and tutor in those things which lead to eternal life. The church should reflect the authority of Christ in its teaching about the truth of Christ. Yet the authority of the church is supremely displayed in its power over evil and unclean spirits. So the prayer of the kingdom, the Lord's prayer, also asks that God's people should be 'delivered' from evil.

Establishing the Bridgehead

And Joshua the son of Nun sent two men secretly from Shittim as spies, saying, 'Go, view the land, especially Jericho.' And they went, and came in to the house of a harlot whose name was Rahab, and lodged there. . . Then the king of Jericho sent to Rahab, saying, 'Bring forth the men that have come to you, who entered your house; for they have come to search out all the land.' But the woman had taken the two men and hidden them; and she said, 'True, men came to me, but I did not know where they came from; and when the gate was to be closed, at dark, the men went out; where the men went I do not know; pursue them quickly, for you will overtake them.' But she had brought them up to the roof, and hid them with the stalks of flax which she had laid in order on the roof.

. . .Before they lay down, she came up to them on the roof, and said to the men, 'I know that the Lord has given you the land, and that the fear of you has fallen upon us, and that all the inhabitants of the land melt away before you. . . Now then, swear to me by the Lord that as I have dealt kindly with you, you also will deal kindly with my father's house, and give me a sure sign, and save alive my father and mother, my brothers and sisters, and all who belong to them, and deliver our lives from death.'   Joshua 2:1, 3−6, 8−9, 12−13

His-story Here is a strange story indeed: a bridgehead is established behind enemy lines in nothing less than a brothel! Rahab knows a thing or two! From her little house in the city wall she has seen something of the surrounding army of Israel. Furthermore, if you want to know anything in an ancient walled city, the gossip at the gate will keep you informed.

So here is a hero of faith! She surveys the scene, weighs the probabilities, takes some soundings and sees which way things are going. She then risks everything on a hunch. If the hunch proves to be right and the city falls to the Israelites not only will she be saved, but all her household.

She has just the same profile as the heroes commended by Jesus in the New Testament in many of his parables. They risk everything and discern which way things are going. She is disloyal to the king of Jericho and his kingdom, because she has caught a glimpse of another kingdom which will overtake and overturn the kingdom of Jericho. She is a hero of faith — perhaps one of the most surprising of God's many, strangely 'J-shaped' people.

The Jesus story For 'faith is the assurance of things hoped for, the conviction of things not seen' (Hebrews 11:1). Since the time of Abraham some men and women have lived that sort of life — almost gambling on the outcome of things. Together with Abraham they have been men and women who have 'walked by faith and not by sight' (2 Corinthians 5:7). The writer of the epistle to the Hebrews praises a long line of such people throughout the ages who have lived in this sort of gambling spirit; or lived by this sort of faith, we may prefer to say. Furthermore the writer of that same epistle is not ashamed to place Rahab in that long line of heroes of faith naming her and praising her apparently, contradictory role. 'By faith Rahab the harlot did not perish with those who were disobedient, because she had given friendly welcome to the spies' (Hebrews 11:31). She had seen which way the wind was blowing and was not ashamed to change her colours accordingly.

As Jesus preaches the inevitable coming of the kingdom in the New Testament he pleads through his parables to God's chosen people to open their eyes and begin to see what God is doing: which way the wind is blowing. The future is no longer with God's ancient people the Jews. It has been taken from them and given to others. In the light of that historical analysis Jesus urges the old Israel to 'make friends for yourselves by means of unrighteous mammon, so that when it fails they may receive you into the eternal habitations' (Luke 16:9). Watch, look and listen, from the ramparts and see what is happening. Then ask yourself where your *ultimate* loyalties lie?

My story 'Who is on the Lord's side?' God needs men and women who are loyal to him *in* the world, yet who are not *of* the world. We need to declare for the Lord not only in church on Sundays where we stand up with God's people to recite the creed and express our faith in a conducive atmosphere. We need to project that faith and loyalty behind enemy lines, where Christ is not known or even perhaps more accurately where he is actually persecuted or ridiculed. We need to express our faith and show our colours between Monday and Saturday in what we like to call our secular job or in our everyday life. Only so will the kingdoms of this world 'become the kingdom of our Lord and of his Christ' (Revelation 11:15).

A Sign of Contradiction

Then (Rahab) let them down by a rope through the window, for her house was built into the city wall, so that she dwelt in the wall. And she said to them, 'Go into the hills, lest the pursuers meet you; and hide yourselves there three days, until the pursuers have returned; then afterward you may go your way.' The men said to her, 'We will be guiltless with respect to this oath of yours which you have made us swear. Behold, when we come into the land, you shall bind this scarlet cord in the window through which you let us down; and you shall gather into your house your father and mother, your brothers, and all your father's household'. . . And she said, 'According to your words, so be it.' Then she sent them away, and they departed; and she bound the scarlet cord in the window.   Joshua 2:15—18, 21

His-story   There was nothing very spiritual about Rahab the harlot, if by spiritual you mean impractical or only concerned with immaterial things. What is spiritual for the Christian, as for the Jew, expresses itself *through* history, *through* matter, the outward, the visible and the tangible. So Rahab declares her faith by showing her courage, and even her imagination! The outward sign and the inward motivation belong together. There is no such thing as secret faith when the chips are down. Rahab expresses her change of heart in both a practical way and in a visible way. So she devises a sign of her faith — that scarlet cord visible from her window. It is a sign of faith and loyalty to new colours, for those with eyes to see.

Previously in the history of Israel, when Moses was preparing to lead God's people out of Egypt there had been another sign for those who were to be saved from the sword of the angel of death. The blood from the passover lamb was daubed over the doorposts of the houses of the children of Israel. The families from the houses so marked were *saved* from the last and most terrible of all the plagues.

Throughout the history of God's ancient people, the covenant and bond between God and his chosen people has been expressed by a visible and tangible sign. In the story of Noah, the new covenant between God and his people aboard the ark is sealed with the outward and visible sign of the rainbow. 'When I bring clouds over the earth, and the bow is seen in the clouds, I will remember my covenant' are the words of promise in the book of Genesis (Genesis 9:14—15). Such signs are frequently practical, colourful and useful. Mundane and ordinary, like circumcision, they signify the covenant and bond which is not just a mystical and spiritual one but rather one which touches every aspect of life — the unseen and the secret made obvious through the outward and the visible.

The Jesus story In the New Testament outward signs and wonders are not given to create faith (cp. John 4:48) but rather they do *accompany* faith. The descent of the dove at the baptism of Jesus at the outset of his ministry and the darkness over the whole land from the sixth to the ninth hour at the close of his earthly ministry are but two of many examples. The veil of the temple was torn from the top to the bottom. Jesus washes the feet of the disciples as a *sign* of servanthood; the bread and the wine at the eucharist are signs of spiritual nutrition. So Christianity embraces the physical and the spiritual and re-shapes and re-orders that physical world. A living faith for an everyday world is expressed *through* works and covenants are sealed *with* signs and symbols. That is what William Temple meant when he said of Christianity that it was of all religions the most materialistic: it is the spiritual expressed *through* the physical.

My story 'In this sign we conquer' was the motto adopted by Constantine when he officially declared the Roman empire to be Christian in AD 313. In Christian marriage a ring or rings are used as outward sign(s) of bonding. In our baptism we are marked for life (literally and symbolically) as the priest prays that we should 'never be ashamed to confess the faith of Christ crucified; fight under his banner against sin the world and the devil and continue Christ's faithful soldiers and servants' to the end of our lives.

Yet the principal sign of Christianity is itself a sign of contradiction — the cross — somewhat J-shaped! To the world it meant death and destruction. For Christians it is the sign of life, liberty and victory. The instrument of shame has become the instrument of glory. *Christus rex* — Jesus our king reigns from the tree.

The Womb and the Tomb

So, when the people set out from their tents, to pass over the Jordan with the priests bearing the ark of the covenant before the people, and when those who bore the ark had come to the Jordan, and the feet of the priests bearing the ark were dipped in the brink of the water (the Jordan overflows all its banks throughout the time of harvest), the waters coming down from above stood and rose up in a heap far off, at Adam, the city that is beside Zarethan, and those flowing down toward the sea of the Arabah, the Salt Sea, were wholly cut off; and the people passed over opposite Jericho. And while all Israel were passing over on dry ground, the priests who bore the ark of the covenant of the Lord stood on dry ground in the midst of the Jordan, until all the nation finished passing over the Jordan.   Joshua 3:14—17

His-story New life begins the other side of water. Water cuts us off, as we say, from the mainland. We pass through it at birth and we are raised up out of it at baptism. It divides kingdoms and has a significant place on the maps of our world.

So here once again the Jews, are to cross over a river (the Jordan) as they had once crossed over the Red Sea. Notice it is the Lord (the Lord of creation and history) who on both occasions makes a way for them.

The Jordan was another turning point for God's people in their long pilgrimage from deliverance out of bondage in Egypt, through the Red Sea and wilderness and now into the land of promise. There is 'one more river to cross — the river of Jordan'.

Water is a basic image throughout the scriptures because it is at the heart of all life. New life begins in the water of the womb. The body is washed before it is placed in the tomb. We take a shower to refresh ourselves to prepare for the day or another part of the day. It is the place of refreshment, cleansing and generally it is clearly and significantly marked on the maps of our lives. In the maps of pilgrimage it is the Lord who gives his people a way *through* the waters, to a chapter of new life, 'cut off' from the old, by rivers or by seas and by oceans.

The Jesus story It is very significant that nearly all the 'signs' in St John's gospel are closely related to water. The gospel begins with the water at Cana of Galilee; the water in the storm, the pool at

Bethzetha, the woman at the well, the washing of the feet of the disciples in the upper room, and even the water and blood coming from the pierced side of the crucified Christ. In all the gospels the early life of discipleship was in, on and around the waters of the Sea of Galilee.

Yes, all new life, as at birth, is the other side of water. Hence Jesus begins his life (as a man) as we all do in the waters of the womb. This is taken up in the symbol of new, abundant life — the life which has literally been *through* it, so that the new life is stronger than death. We undergo the waters of affliction without finally going under! We call that baptism. Baptism was used before Christ by John the Baptizer and by the Essenes. It was the symbol of cleansing or refreshment but also the symbol for a new start — a new life — a second birth.

Jesus takes all this a step further. He links baptism with the whole complex of what he went through and what he underwent — his passion, death and resurrection: 'Are you able to drink the cup that I drink, or to be baptized with the baptism with which I am baptized?' (Mark 10:38). In some way baptism and death are linked. St Paul links them finally and inseparably. God's new people are people who have passed through it. They are God's 'Red Sea people'. We have been baptized with Christ, submerged with him in the closest possible identification with him and the new life, together with all those other J-shaped people who have undergone without finally going under! Then we have been raised with him. St Paul can confidently assert: 'We were buried therefore with him by baptism into death, so that as Christ was raised from the dead by the glory of the Father, we too might walk in newness of life' (Romans 6:4).

My story   Christians are J-shaped: they have indeed been *through* it — more perhaps than most. They have been baptized once, but they have 'died' daily! The recovered alcoholic has been down to the bottom, where he knows 'he is powerless' over drink. He is then raised up by a strength which is not his own.

Real life (abundant life, or eternal life) only begins when we are literally out of our depth. For then we have to be raised up by a power which is clearly not our own. The brave new life in the brave new world is for those men and women who, like Christopher Columbus, are so secure at the centre that they dare to go to the edges in the knowledge that underneath are the everlasting arms of love.

'Jesu, be thou our constant Guide;   Bid Jordan's narrow stream divide,
Then, when the word is given,   And bring us safe to heaven.'

(Charles Wesley)

The Power of the Word

Then Joshua rose early in the morning, and the priests took up the ark of the Lord. And the seven priests bearing the seven trumpets of rams' horns before the ark of the Lord passed on, blowing the trumpets continually; and the armed men went before them, and the rear guard came after the ark of the Lord, while the trumpets blew continually. And the second day they marched around the city once, and returned into the camp. So they did for six days.

On the seventh day they rose early at the dawn of day, and marched around the city in the same manner seven times: it was only on that day that they marched around the city seven times. And at the seventh time, when the priests had blown the trumpets, Joshua said to the people, 'Shout; for the Lord has given you the city'. . . So the people shouted, and the trumpets were blown. As soon as the people heard the sound of the trumpet, the people raised a great shout, and the wall fell down flat, so that the people went up into the city, every man straight before him, and they took the city.   Joshua 6:12—16, 20

His-story 'Shout; for the Lord has given you the city.' This was strange warfare indeed. Yet God's people have to learn from beginning to end the nature of their true identity. They are God's people. What is done is done *through* them. It is God's strength working *through* their weakness.

That is not the same as quietism. In quietism we are tempted to assume that there is nothing for us to do: that God will do it all. That is wrong. Pelagianism is the opposite error. It suggests that we do it all in our own strength, with *our* talents and *our* unaided skills. Both are opposing errors lying at the extreme and opposite ends of the whole truth. The truth of the scriptures and the witness of the church is an even more wonderful chemistry:

Without God, we cannot;

without us, he will not.

(St Augustine)

So with God, the Israelites could not have taken the great city of Jericho which was one of the finest fortified cities of the ancient world and noted in contemporary chronicles for its impregnable walls. Yet God did not simply accomplish a divine fiat — out of the blue, as we say. Indeed the Israelites are engaged together with God in this strange ritual of surrounding the walls of the city and then with a word — God's word — assailing the city.

The Jesus story In the New Testament we see Jesus as teacher, example, physician, friend. We also see him as victor and Lord of the hosts of God's army. For the New Testament assumes that life is a battle and a struggle of forces. The Christian is called upon to be a warrior in the army of the Lord. It is not a popular image in our day, for all kinds of good reasons, and it is clearly an image which needs tempering alongside other less militant images of Jesus in the scriptures.

Nevertheless, the battle between good and evil rages and will never rage more savagely than just before the end of all things. The war in heaven recorded in Revelation has its counterpart on earth. The Lord has given to his church and to his people the deeds and the words with which to fight this battle. So Jesus, the new Joshua, tells his disciples and his troops; 'No one can enter a strong man's house and plunder his goods, unless he first binds the strong man; then indeed he may plunder his house' (Mark 3:27).

My story Deliverance from evil is part of the Lord's own prayer. We are bidden to bind and to loose on earth and if this is done in his name it will have eternal repercussions in the war of heaven. We would do much better in our discipleship if we would sometimes see it for what it is — a war against evil; and if we would see the sacraments and the word of scripture for what they truly are — the weapons which the devil simply cannot withstand.

There is power alike in word and sacrament. There is a stern warning in the New Testament, that there would arise a church which had the 'form' of true religion but without its 'power' (2 Timothy 3:5). We can dress up, look the part and shout the right slogans, but remain powerless over evil — of no earthly use to the Lord in his warfare against evil. The word of God is only at its most powerful when it is on the lips of an obedient heart and will. All kinds of walls and barriers fall flat before that Word, whether it is shouted or whispered — that still small voice of the inner life.

——————— One for All ———————

And Joshua said to the two men who had spied out the land, 'Go into the harlot's house, and bring out from it the woman, and all who belong to her, as you swore to her.' So the young men who had been spies went in, and brought out Rahab, and her father and mother and brothers and all who belonged to her; and they brought all her kindred, and set them outside the camp of Israel. And they burned the city with fire, and all within it; only the silver and gold, and the vessels of bronze and of iron, they put into the treasury of the house of the Lord. But Rahab the harlot, and her father's household, and all who belonged to her, Joshua saved alive; and she dwelt in Israel to this day, because she hid the messengers whom Joshua sent to spy out Jericho.   Joshua 6:22—25

His-story   'So the young men who had been spies went in and brought out Rahab and her father and mother and brothers and all who belonged to her; and they brought all her kindred, and set them outside the camp of Israel.' The many are saved by the few; as the few are saved by the one. We see here again, as frequently in other places in the Old Testament, the corporate nature of faith. The faith of the few can affect the many as the disobedience of the few can affect the many. The Bible is not a book about individualistic pietism. It is the word of God's plan to save (if possible) the whole world.

We must remember the story of Abraham's plea for Sodom. Here we see Abraham as the priestly person — that is to say as the man for others. He pleads with the Lord for the city of Sodom. He asks the Lord, in true intercessory prayer: 'Suppose there are fifty righteous within the city; wilt thou then destroy the place and not spare it for the fifty righteous who are in it? Far be it from thee to do such a thing, to slay the righteous with the wicked.' Slowly Abraham wittles the Lord down to ten — and the Lord answers: 'For the sake of ten I will not destroy it' (Genesis 18:23—32). There was one moment in history when in fact there was only one righteous man and for his sake — for the sake of Jesus Christ — the potential is at hand for the salvation of the whole world.

So I am my brother's keeper and both my evil deeds as well as my faith affect others. God's people have in that sense always been a priestly people — men and women for others, not individualists just for themselves. In the Kingdom competition is replaced by interdependence.

The Jesus story So Paul is adamant: 'As in Adam all die, so also in Christ shall all be made alive' (1 Corinthians 15:22). As by one man sin entered the world, so by one Man grace entered the world — in fact through a woman (Mary)! So Paul speaks of the body of sin as well as of the body of Christ. Both alike, however, are a body.

Little wonder therefore in the book of the Acts of the Apostles, when the Philippi gaoler declares for Jesus Christ and is baptized, we are told that 'all his household' was baptized with him (Acts 16). That would include children as well as possibly slaves. In other words all those to whom he was bound in loyalty — all those for whom in some sense he was responsible. All of them are caught up in his faith. So in the gospel, it is quite clear that Jesus healed the paralytic, not so much on account of his faith, but quite explicitly on account of the faith of the four men who carried the paralytic to Jesus (Mark 2:5). This is a classic example of intercession. Rahab is acting here with all God's chosen people — chosen not for personal privilege, but for the sake of others to whom she is bonded in love and concern. Such is the nature of true intercession and priesthood. It is essentially life for others, as opposed to 'every man for himself'.

My story To be a godparent and to pledge our faith for others is the most priestly and indeed the most Christlike act we shall possibly ever be asked to do. The church is a priestly community, not a self-serving club, and as such exists essentially for the sake of those who are not members of it. I was baptized for nothing less than to be Jesus Christ for others — in that sense I am a Christian. Christ 'always lives to make intercession' (Hebrews 7:25). He lives for the world as surely as he died for it. God needs men and women to live for the world, just as much as he needs men and women who are ready to die for the gospel.

—— Covenant or Contract? ——

But Joshua said to the people, 'You cannot serve the Lord; for he is a holy God; he is a jealous God; he will not forgive your transgressions or your sins. If you forsake the Lord and serve foreign gods, then he will turn and do you harm, and consume you, after having done you good.' And the people said to Joshua, 'Nay; but we will serve the Lord.' Then Joshua said to the people, 'You are witnesses against yourselves that you have chosen the Lord, to serve him.' And they said, 'We are witnesses.' He said, 'Then put away the foreign gods which are among you, and incline your heart to the Lord, the God of Israel.' And the people said to Joshua, 'The Lord our God we will serve, and his voice we will obey.' So Joshua made a covenant with the people that day, and made statutes and ordinances for them at Shechem. And Joshua wrote these words in the book of the law of God; and he took a great stone, and set it up there under the oak in the sanctuary of the Lord.

Joshua 24:19—26

His-story 'If you forsake the Lord and serve foreign gods, then he will turn and do you harm and consume you,' warns Joshua as he prepares to seal the covenant. The wrath of God in the Old Testament is a difficult but an important concept. It is not God getting angry and hating us. Rather it is what happens when his constant love is rejected. God loves his ancient people and is bound to them in covenant — a covenant which cannot be broken. If God's people are unfaithful, the covenant is not like a contract. It is not then dissolved and rendered ineffective. What was there for good when the covenant was first accepted becomes destructive when we are unfaithful to that commitment.

God's love does not become neutral and ineffective. It warms us if we relate to it properly (like fire) but if we go against it, it consumes and destroys us. So Joshua sets up a stone as a reminder of that covenant. The Jews will need to return to a place again and again in order to re-affirm their faith — a place with a sign. Whenever they have fallen, it will be the re-affirmed covenant which will raise them up — the promises of the covenant made on that day with Joshua and all God's people.

The Jesus story 'It is a fearful thing to fall into the hands of the living God' (Hebrews 10:31). God's love for us is all powerful. It is wonderful when we respond to it positively but terrible and destructive if we kick against it ('It hurts you to kick against the goads', Paul is cautioned — Acts 26:14). So Jesus tells us that we shall be broken and re-ordered by God's covenanted love for us but much worse is it for those who, once in covenant, reject that love. 'Every one that falls on that stone will be broken to pieces; but when it falls on any one it will crush them' (Luke 20:18).

My story Hell then is not that state or place where God ceases to love me. Would perhaps that it were! No, hell is that state or place where God loves me as he always has done and always will — but my response is 'No'. That is hell for me and I experience the wrath of God (you can see it written large across people's faces)!

Purgatory is not that state or place where God ceases to love me. It is that state or place where God loves me but I simply cannot make up my mind (it is the place where most of us spend most of our time). Heaven is that state or place where God loves me, neither more nor less than he always has and always will ('O love that will not let me go'). Just for a moment (perhaps at my Communion or in prayer) but always by his grace, like Mary the mother of the Lord, there are moments when I can say, 'Yes, amen; Let it be to me. . .' For a moment, that is heaven on earth! In baptism we are literally marked for life and sealed by the Holy Spirit in the covenant of God's love. We need to recall our baptism frequently, especially when we are cast down, so that it may raise us up. That is why the whole church reaffirms baptismal vows at the feast of the Resurrection — Eastertide.

But we need to reaffirm our baptismal vows at all the turning points of our lives. We cannot renew them because they do not run out. It is reaffirmation that is needed in such a covenant, which is certainly not a contract. God loves us by covenant and with total commitment and so that is the way that he would have us learn to love others.

'Alone, O Love ineffable,
Thy saving name is given;
To turn aside from thee is hell,
To walk with thee is heaven.
                    (John Whittier)
'In the end perhaps there are only two alternatives: "Consumed by fire, or by fire." ' (T.S. Eliot)

JOSEPH: THE VICTIM

PERHAPS no other Old Testament character, in his story of unjust suffering accompanied by a total forgiveness of his persecutors, so foreshadows the person of Jesus Christ, as does Joseph — the eleventh son of Jacob and the elder son of Rachel, Jacob's favoured wife. As the story is narrated, Joseph's sufferings, like those of Jesus in the New Testament, served only to prepare him for 'the glory that should follow' (1 Peter 1:11). Like Jesus in the New Testament, this Joseph is the special, beloved and 'unique' son in some special sense for his father Jacob. After all he was 'the son of his old age' and we are told that Jacob loved him more than 'any of his children'. It was as though from his birth that Joseph was marked out to be different and special — hence the gift from his father of the special long robe with sleeves. He was a dreamer, and an interpreter of dreams — a man of intuition, sensitivity and deep spiritual awareness. In one single day he was raised from the prison cell to be Prime Minister of Egypt and to be the right hand man of Pharaoh. Joseph was dramatically a J-shaped person in whose life-story and destiny we see salvation for many others at work.

Not unnaturally, the psalmist likes to tell Joseph's story and to sing it as he recalls the hand of God at work in and through this attractive, Old Testament figure. 'He sent a man before them — Joseph, sold as a slave. They bruised his feet with shackles, his neck was put in irons, till what he foretold came to pass, till the word of the Lord proved him true. The king sent and released him, the ruler of peoples set him free. He made him master of his household, ruler over all he possessed' (Psalm 105:17−21 NIV).

So in the same vein, St Peter could affirm this same theme continuously in his early preaching of Jesus and the resurrection, when he used such phrases as 'this Jesus, God raised up' (Acts 2:32) and 'God having raised up his servant' (Acts 3:26). Yet again, and perhaps most conclusively, 'Let all the house of Israel therefore know assuredly, that God has made him both Lord and Christ, this Jesus whom you crucified' (Acts 2:36). As in the story of Joseph, we are Christ's brothers who have put down Jesus, but whom God has raised up and highly exalted. God has given him the name that is above every name — to sit at his right hand and reign in glory. The 'Author of life', whom we have killed, God has 'raised from the dead' (Acts 3:15).

In Joseph then we see the supremely J-shaped, servant figure in the Old Testament. It is a theme which is taken up and amplified by Isaiah in the servant songs and most clearly and ultimately identified with Jesus himself — the true suffering servant — in the New Testament. Jesus did not come to lord it over his brethren. Indeed in his own words he came 'not to be served but to serve, and to give his life as a ransom for many' (Matthew 20:28). The very name Joseph gives the clue, for it means — 'may (God) add (posterity)'. By life (Joseph's life) laid down, the eleventh son of Jacob saved the lives of all his brethren and his father, their children and their children's children. Jesus is adamant in the New Testament that no one takes his life from him but that he willingly lays it down (John 10:18). In the stocks in prison there can be no doubt that Joseph needed time to move from a position of resenting his fate to a position of going out to meet it and to turn it to advantage. So it is that in the end good comes out of evil and Joseph is able to greet his guilty brethren with words of forgiveness and loving acceptance. We see in Joseph the acorn of redemptive suffering already at work, ultimately growing to its full size in God's time in the tree of Calvary and in the redemptive sufferings of Jesus Christ in the New Testament.

Questions for Discussion and Reflection

1.   'When the worship is ended, the service begins.' In what ways are worship and service in the community related?

2.   In what ways do the wounds of the past imprison us in present behaviour patterns? How can we break out of these prisons?

3.   What is the priesthood of all believers?

A Uniform of Service

> Jacob dwelt in the land of his father's sojournings, in the land of Canaan. This is the history of the family of Jacob.
>
> Joseph, being seventeen years old, was shepherding the flock with his brothers; he was a lad with the sons of Bilhah and Zilpah, his father's wives; and Joseph brought an ill report of them to their father. Now Israel loved Joseph more than any other of his children, because he was the son of his old age; and he made him a long robe with sleeves. But when his brothers saw that their father loved him more than all his brothers, they hated him, and could not speak peaceably to him.
>
> Genesis 37:1–4

His-story The Old Testament picture of Joseph at seventeen is sufficiently clear for us to glean that he belongs to those special people, anointed by God and set apart — in some sense, unique. They stand out as special sons, like Isaac or David. We recognize such figures first because they are *given* in a characteristic way, as was Isaac to Abraham and Sarah. As so often, the child of old age (they are both parents clearly beyond ordinary child-bearing), Isaac is referred to as their son, their 'only son'. For parents of such an age he is a special gift from God. (In fact he has to be a sort of joke, for they are *so* old — hence his name 'Isaac', which literally means laughter or a joke.) 'Take your son, your only son Isaac, whom you love', the Lord says to Abraham (Genesis 22:2). The word used in the Greek version of the Old Testament (Septuagint) is '*agapētos*'. It is translated 'beloved', therefore 'unique, special or only' son.

The Jesus story It is the same word as we see used in the New Testament at the baptism of Jesus: 'This is my beloved (*agapētos*) son'. In another place, the classic text concerning our redemption tells us that God so loved the world that he gave us 'his *only begotten* son' (John 3:16). Again, the word occurs in Mark and Luke's parable of the vineyard: 'The owner of the vineyard said, "What shall I do? I will send my *beloved* son"' (Luke 20:13). So it is that the prophetic and priestly figures whom God has sent in past times — given as special gifts through the ages — have finally come to their perfection in the ultimate and sacrificial figure of the gift of Jesus, 'the only begotten son' of the Father.

It is interesting that that particular phrase ('the only begotten son') is especially Johannine, occurring no less than four times in the gospel of John and four times in the first epistle — perhaps by that same John who may have been the special and beloved disciple.

Once again it is in John that Jesus is especially sketched as the sacrificial figure. In John's treatment of the events, and even the dating, of Good Friday, Jesus dies at the same time and on the same day as the Passover Lamb. That animal was traditionally prefigured by the ram sacrifice which God provided in place of none other than Isaac (Genesis 22:7–8, 13), that original 'agapētos'.

Now we can see perhaps how Joseph belongs to that long line of special, beloved and only sons who are provided straight from the heart of Love himself— God's own special, beloved Son. (Is it too fanciful to point out also that it is St John in the fourth gospel, with his special understanding of the sacrificial role of Jesus and in his special friendship with Jesus, who speaks to us of another 'robe' — one without seams? Is this the New Testament version of the cloak of Joseph in the Old Testament given to the special son by the Father?)

My story Whatever it is about those specially chosen as God's J-shaped people, one thing is clear. They are chosen not for privilege, but for service; not for personal salvation only but for the part they play in the salvation of others. Of those to whom much is given much will be required (Luke 12:48). The church is richly graced and generously anointed with the Holy Spirit. Yet the Holy Spirit is given not simply for the renewal of the church. Renewal by the Holy Spirit must issue in mission, service and evangelism. We are richly clothed in the robe of Christ — the same Christ who laid aside his garments and took a towel to wash the feet of his disciples. In the early church at baptism you put on the robe of Christ. Yet in some sense baptism is ordination to the diaconate — marked for life — a life of service and sacrifice.

The Redemption of Religion

. . . So Joseph went after his brothers, and found them at Dothan. They saw him afar off, and before he came near to them they conspired against him to kill him. They said to one another, 'Here comes this dreamer. Come now, let us kill him and throw him into one of the pits; then we shall say that a wild beast has devoured him, and we shall see what will become of his dreams.' But when Reuben heard it, he delivered him out of their hands, saying, 'Let us not take his life.' And Reuben said to them, 'Shed no blood; cast him into this pit here in the wilderness, but lay no hand upon him' — that he might rescue him out of their hand, to restore him to his father. So when Joseph came to his brothers, they stripped him of his robe, the long robe with sleeves that he wore; and they took him and cast him into a pit. . . Then Midianite traders passed by; and they drew Joseph up and lifted him out of the pit, and sold him to the Ishmaelites for twenty shekels of silver; and they took Joseph to Egypt.   Genesis 37:17—24, 28

His-story So Joseph is betrayed by his own brothers and sold for twenty shekels of silver into slavery. Clearly his brothers were jealous of him and plotted even to take his life.

The story of betrayal and plotting against the servants of God is a constant theme throughout the Old Testament. Frequently the enemies of the friends of God are from within the household of the family of faith — within the family of God itself. Nearly all the J-shaped people we are reflecting upon were put down by those who professed faith. The true prophet (such as Jeremiah) is attacked by the false prophets but all of course (ironically) in the name of Yahweh.

Truth to tell, unredeemed religion feeds perhaps the bloodiest of all motives in history. The Old Testament is a very sad record of religious wars, bloodshed, hatred and jealousy and nearly always in the name of Yahweh and righteousness. If ever we are tempted to believe that religion is good or at least harmless we have only to read the record of the Old Testament! Religion, love, the family — all need redeeming. While they frequently show humanity at its best we must remember that the perversion of the best is also the worst. The devil is an angel — but a fallen angel. Happily that is not the last word however. For the saint is the forgiven, restored and resurrected sinner. Religion itself needs reshaping and it is the J-shaped people in and through whose life-stories that we see religion being reshaped, restored and redeemed.

The Jesus story In the New Testament it is from within the apostolic band of those closest to Jesus that the betrayer is to be found — Judas. The second name, Iscariot, could suggest that he was a member of the Zealot party. He would have been jealous for his nation and for religion. He wanted to make Jesus serve his ends — to bend the movement of Jesus to forward his (Judas') purposes: he wanted Jesus to follow him and not the other way round.

Of course he was a religious man and did what he did (sold Jesus for thirty pieces of silver) probably for the highest religious and nationalistic motives. The same is true in a different way of Caiaphas. Nearly all those who betrayed Jesus and handed him over to death were religious people. Their religion was a religion which was perverted and bent to serve their own ends.

Judas wanted to serve a leader who would lead in the direction Judas wanted. He wanted to serve under the strength of powerful leadership. Instead Jesus (and also Joseph), as instruments of God's redeeming purposes, had first to undergo weakness in order to be raised up by another's strength. Thus it is that such J-shaped people glorify neither themselves nor a cause, but only the true and living God — 'who putteth down one and raiseth up another'.

My story How often do I betray Jesus by seeking to champion a cause or an ideology, be it right wing or left? Am I really ready to follow a failure (in human terms) — the crucified — and be baptized with his baptism and drink of his cup? The church at its strongest in history, when it has most wielded political power, has generally been most corrupt. At such times it has nearly always persecuted the 'Josephs' of God in the name of God.

Judas then is an essential part of the record of God's J-shaped people. Because he could not bend he was finally broken. He was literally hoisted by his own petard. He was possibly the victim of high ideals for a cause for which in the end he was willing to sacrifice even a person. He was not able to repent and to be shaped into the profile of life. That always involves tears. Peter (after his betrayal) went out and wept bitterly; Judas, he went out and hanged himself. Tillich was right: 'Jesus Christ came to save us from religion.'

The Passion of Joseph

Now Joseph was taken down to Egypt, and Potiphar, an officer of Pharaoh, the captain of the guard, an Egyptian, bought him from the Ishmaelites who had brought him down there. The Lord was with Joseph, and he became a successful man; and he was in the house of his master the Egyptian, and his master saw that the Lord was with him, and that the Lord caused all that he did to prosper in his hands. So Joseph found favour in his sight and attended him, and he made him overseer of his house and put him in charge of all that he had. . .

But one day, when (Joseph) went into the house to do his work and none of the men of the house was there in the house, she (his master's wife) caught him by his garment, saying 'Lie with me'. But he left his garment in her hand, and fled and got out of the house. . . Then she laid up his garment by her until his master came home, and she told him the. . . story, saying, 'The Hebrew servant, whom you have brought among us, came in to me to insult me; but as soon as I lifted up my voice and cried, he left his garment with me, and fled out of the house.'

When his master heard the words which his wife spoke to him, 'This is the way your servant treated me', his anger was kindled. And Joseph's master took him and put him into the prison, the place where the king's prisoners were confined, and he was there in prison.

Genesis 39:1−4, 11−12, 16−20

His-story Here is the story of the 'Passion' of Joseph. It is worth noting at this stage that in the story of Joseph we are not regaled with impressive accounts of what Joseph did and what Joseph did next. We are not presented with the acts of Joseph! In this part of the narrative it is not so much a matter of what Joseph did, but rather more of what was done to Joseph, what others did to him. It is not so much where he went, as what he underwent. He is led like a lamb to the slaughter. Through his sufferings Joseph was hollowed out and emptied out. The story now begins to be the account of what the Lord did *through* Joseph. J-shaped people are intended to become channels of God's loving, redemptive activity. As such they give God a foothold into the world of everyday life. God is present *in* and *through* his people.

There is one inevitable result; evil automatically reacts to the positive presence of God. Potiphar's wife inevitably came into confrontation with Joseph. The war in heaven between good and evil must be fought out *in* history and God's J-shaped people are inevitably always in the front line of that battle. Nice, harmless people are somehow not quite so involved in all that sort of confrontation. Of course, they have not much of a story to tell! History is made not between those kind of people, but rather between the two front lines of good and evil. It is a fascinating story which rings true to life — life on the frontier. Joseph found himself there. It was all part of what he had to undergo. It was his true 'Passion'.

The Jesus story 'Emmanuel' literally means God with us. In the fourth gospel especially, the writer is at pains to point out that everything that Jesus does is done in the power of, and in obedience to, the Father.

It is inevitable therefore that Jesus draws evil to himself — or rather he draws out the evil. People cannot be indifferent to Jesus — they either follow him or try to stone him. The evil spirits shout at him. By his incarnation he has drawn the battle lines out of eternity into time and into history — out of heaven, to earth — and he earths the battle in and through himself, as lightning is earthed.

W. H. Vanstone, in his book *The Stature of Waiting*, suggests that once Jesus is *handed over* by Judas in the garden of Gethsemane that the narrative changes (especially in the synoptic gospels) and that once again (as with Joseph) we are not told so much what Jesus did or did next; but rather what was done to Jesus. After his arrest in the garden, Jesus is seldom the subject of an active verb. He is rather the object of others' actions. This is his Passion. Justice is perverted as with Joseph; evil is drawn out as they not only deny the truth of his words, but buffet and seek to disfigure the beauty of his face.

My story Those who are chosen specially by God as vehicles of his loving activity inevitably enter into something of the mystery of the Passion of Christ. They are not passive people: rather they are passionate people, *through* whom God's love enters the world. At the same time, and through the same door, that same love is in combat with evil in time, in history and in space. All such wars focus in the Passion and Death of Jesus. It is no accident that the saints of God seem to have more than their fair share of suffering and martyrdom. For to witness is essentially to be a martyr. It is no accident that they are the same word in Greek. Joseph and Jesus witness to God's presence with them: the tragedy in their stories is no unfortunate accident. Rather it is the way things are and necessarily it is the shape of things to come. For in the end this is the way evil is defeated, drawn out, and spent. And all this is accomplished in and through the Passion of

Christ — and also in and through all those who share in some way in the mystery of his redemptive suffering: all the other J-shaped people.

The Foolishness of God

After two whole years, Pharaoh dreamed that he was standing by the Nile, and behold, there came up out of the Nile seven cows sleek and fat, and they fed in the reed grass. And behold, seven other cows, gaunt and thin, came up out of the Nile after them, and stood by the other cows on the bank of the Nile. And the gaunt and thin cows ate up the seven sleek and fat cows. And Pharaoh awoke. And he fell asleep and dreamed a second time; and behold, seven ears of grain, plump and good, were growing on one stalk. And behold, after them sprouted seven ears, thin and blighted by the east wind. And the thin ears swallowed up the seven plump and full ears. And Pharaoh awoke, and behold, it was a dream. So in the morning his spirit was troubled; and he sent and called for all the magicians of Egypt and all its wise men; and Pharaoh told them his dream, but there was none who could interpret it to Pharaoh.

Genesis 41:1—8

His-story The Bible is not a book about God. Rather it is a book about the mighty acts of God in and through history. The Bible does not attempt the impossible: namely, to describe with finite language the indescribable person of the infinite God who is beyond our furthest knowledge. In that way the Bible avoids the classical pitfall of all religious language — namely, of making God in our own image. So we do not see the face of God in the scriptures. Rather we see the hand of God in events — what we sometimes call the saving acts of God. There is the deliverance of the Israelites out of Egypt; the plagues; the passage through the Red Sea; the siege of Jerusalem by Sennacherib in 701 BC. These are in some sense events of history. Some would see them simply as accidents of history and others discern God's loving purposes at work in and *through* them. Christians insist on seeing God's hand at work through history and supremely and ultimately in the death and resurrection of Jesus Christ.

So in the story of Pharaoh's dreams we see the wisdom of the ancient world being made to look foolish while the foolishness of Joseph turns out to be the real wisdom: the wisdom of discernment. One of the ways *into* time and into events and history is through the phenomenon of dreams. The door of the subconscious is often left unlocked at night and it is in sleep (as in panic, fear or breakdown) that God can break into conscious history and recountable history. The first step through that door is into our world of dreams. These 'events' demand interpretation, as indeed do all events. They demand discernment if life is to be rescued from the incidental and the accidental and be given the purpose and shape of providence.

Clever, intellectual prowess is often rendered foolish in this kind of laboratory. Wisdom or discernment is a gift of God. It reflects upon the mind of God. Worldly wisdom through the looking-glass of the record of God's story seems like a mad hatter's tea party — for those who have not the eyes to see. Only wisdom and discernment as a gift of God, rather than an acquired talent, can make sense of God's world in God's way. Hence only Joseph is able to see the hand of God at work in the otherwise meaningless dreams of Pharaoh. He discerns providence all *among* the accidents.

The Jesus story 'Unless you turn and become like children, you will never enter the kingdom of heaven', said Jesus (Matthew 18:3). The wise men in St Matthew's gospel (ch. 2) bring all the worldly learning of the ancients to the feet of the Christ Child in what is the climax and consummation of all education and learning — namely, worship. Worship transcends the intellect — it does not seek to by-pass it. Christianity is not a mindless faith, but it does demand at some point that we set at nought all our learning in order that we may truly have, as a gift, 'the mind of Christ'. That demands a conversion of the mind. Jesus brings a J-shape to the profile of reality with a distinctive and different discernment of worldly value-judgements. 'None of the rulers of this age understood this' (1 Corinthians 2:8). And again St Paul reminds us. 'The foolishness of God is wiser than the wisdom of men' (1 Corinthians 1:25).

My story It is just as possible to see the mind of the creator in the creation as it is possible to see the hand of God in history, but only for those who know what to look for and who have eyes to see. They are 'God's spies', as Shakespeare calls them — his undercover agents who can crack the code. They are the childlike. They are the famous detective heroes — the Miss Marples or M. Poirots of detective-literature, who appear foolish and confused.

The contemplatives then are J-shaped. They have seen right *through* everything and everybody. Yet they are not cynical, for on the *other* side they discern the features of a God of loving purpose — the God of history and the God of eternal significance.

Joseph had to go to the bottom of the class in the school of ancient wisdom only to find that he ended up 'top of the class' with the gift of discernment. So Joseph is clearly in another class altogether. 'God is revealed to us,' says St Paul, 'through the Spirit. For the Spirit searches everything, even the depths of God. . . and we impart this in words not taught by human wisdom but taught by the Spirit' (1 Corinthians 2:10, 13). 'I will destroy the wisdom of the wise and the cleverness of the clever I will thwart' (1 Corinthians 1:19).

— Upside Down —

So Pharaoh said to Joseph, 'Since God has shown you all this, there is none so discreet and wise as you are; you shall be over my house, and all my people shall order themselves as you command; only as regards the throne will I be greater than you.' And Pharaoh said to Joseph, 'Behold, I have set you over all the land of Egypt.' Then Pharaoh took his signet ring from his hand and put it on Joseph's hand, and arrayed him in garments of fine linen, and put a gold chain about his neck; and he made him to ride in his second chariot; and they cried before him, 'Bow the knee!' Thus he set him over all the land of Egypt.

Genesis 41:39–43

His-story Pharaoh recognized in Joseph the spirit of God, revealing to Joseph that which all the training and intellectual brilliance of Pharaoh's professionals could not perceive for themselves or through their own skills and sciences. In the darkness of the prison, Joseph had learned to see by another light — the light of the spirit, which no darkness can overcome. Joseph was truly enlightened.

So in a day — a day of 'resurrection' — Joseph is *raised up* from being a condemned prisoner to being a freedman in the land of Egypt — Prime Minister to King Pharaoh. What a reversal! What a turn up for the books!

Pharaoh, however, recognizes that 'flesh and blood' have not revealed this knowledge and interpretation to Joseph. 'Since God has shown you all this,' exclaims Pharaoh. This interpretation of Joseph's is more than skilful speculation. It is necessarily revelation.

Then, in language which is powerfully regal, Pharaoh makes Joseph his right-hand man — literally his Prime Minister. It is an astonishing reversal of all Joseph's fortunes yet in a strange way everything in Joseph's earlier life has prepared him for this moment. He is given a ring of authority, fine clothes in relation to which even the fine robe given to him by his father, Israel (Jacob) now would seem a poor and pale second-best. With a chain around his neck, Joseph is bound only to Pharaoh the king and he is seated at the king's right hand sharing in his majesty as the crowd shout, 'Bow the knee'.

The Jesus story It is hard to know where to end as we look at the parallels between Joseph and Jesus. 'Flesh and blood has not revealed this to you,' says Jesus at Caesarea Philippi to Peter, 'but my Father who is in heaven' (Matthew 16:17). Faith in Christ is always at root revelation before it is speculation. God gives us his spirit after emptying out our pride and self-sufficiency. Jesus is glorified wherever the Holy Spirit is given (John 7:39) and Jesus is raised up and confessed as Lord. So we must recall yet again that Christ did not rise from the dead as some sort of superman. Jesus died and was raised up by the power of the Father. 'All authority' (not only in Egypt but) 'in heaven and earth' was given to Jesus by the Father (Matthew 28:18). 'He is seated at the right hand of the Father.' God's servant in the end is raised up on 'the third day' as the Prime Minister of the church and the universe. Authority and service belong together at the very right hand of God himself.

This is indeed a roller-coaster pattern! He who was cast down unjustly has been raised up and justified.

My story I find 'in Christ' that the destiny of Joseph and my story are all part of a seamless robe. Cast down and imprisoned by sin, I am emptied and filled with his Spirit. This Spirit alone empowers me by revelation to recognize and confess Jesus as Lord to the glory of God the Father.

Justified by that faith (itself a gift from a loving Father), in Christ by my baptism, clothed in the robe of his righteousness, I am raised to the life of heaven in communion with all the saints — all those other J-shaped people. But notice: my last state of sanctity is even more wonderful than my first state of innocency — before the Fall, before we got into all this business. Having been made 'a little lower than the angels' (Hebrews 2:9), I am raised up in Christ above the angels and given a resurrection body which makes me no longer cling to the poor tailoring of this earthly body, even at its best.

'Amazing grace (how sweet the sound)
That saved a wretch like me!'

(John Newton)

— A Man for All Seasons! —

Before the year of famine came, Joseph had two sons, whom Asenath, the daughter of Potiphera priest of On, bore to him. Joseph called the name of the first-born Manasseh, 'For,' he said, 'God has made me forget all my hardship and all my father's house.' The name of the second he called Ephraim, 'For God has made me fruitful in the land of my affliction.'

The seven years of plenty that prevailed in the land of Egypt came to an end; and the seven years of famine began to come, as Joseph had said. There was famine in all lands; but in all the land of Egypt there was bread.   Genesis 41:50—54

His-story   The seven years of plenty begin to draw to a close, yet Joseph had prepared Egypt for the seven lean years which were to follow. For Joseph history and chronology are reversed! He has been through *his* lean years — the hidden years of slavery, hard labour and imprisonment. Joseph already has his story to tell. He is now a man for all seasons. In the days of his captivity the words of the psalmist would sit well on the lips of Joseph.

'Blessed is the man whose strength is in thee:
in whose heart are thy ways.
Who going through the vale of misery use it for a well:
and the pools are filled with water.'

(Psalm 84:5—6, Coverdale)

In the Revised Standard Version the vale of misery is translated as the valley of Baca — the most God-forsaken, deserted and dry spot on earth. It was in fact the last place that you would ever hope to find springs of water — let alone 'living water'. And yet it is in that stage of Joseph's life that he really found faith. For in the geography of the heart it was in the lean years of imprisonment and degradation that Joseph had found faith and strength. Such people as Joseph literally 'go from strength to strength' (Psalm 84:7).

So he calls his children by names which record for his posterity the story of his story. Both names are signposts for Joseph on the spiritual highway of discipleship. Joseph has put behind him the hardships and pains of his early life (Manasseh); furthermore it was in the very same location where he had experienced affliction and hardship (Egypt) that he had discovered a fruitful life — hence Ephraim. All this must necessarily have been the work of grace and divine healing. So often it is the painful moments from our early life which hold us back from growing up and overcoming them. In nature, painful past events have a strange power to fixate us and arrest our development.

The Jesus story It is in the desert, the God-forsaken place, that Jesus prepares for his fruitful ministry. He was in the desert for forty days and forty nights. He found strength and power there in God alone and we are told that the 'angels ministered to him'. Again at the end of his ministry on earth it was on Calvary Hill, when Jesus could not move, nailed to a cross, that his ministry was most fruitful as he forgave and redeemed the world. After all, it is not for nothing that the church has persisted in calling it Good Friday. Like Joseph, we can, if we will, find the good news all among the bad news — the last place on earth we might ever expect to find it.

My story Joseph experienced the contradiction of the gospel at its most powerful. We do not need to let the pains and afflictions of our early life imprison us indefinitely, discolouring the present and for ever deforming the future. We are told to pray — 'deliver us from evil'. Evil has the power to imprison us in the past; God can give us the grace to unlock that prison and throw open the prison doors. But that is the work of grace alone and it bears no relation whatever, thank God, to our nature, our virtue, or our own strength.

In the land of our affliction we are also able by God's grace to have nevertheless a fruitful life. The music of the deaf Beethoven is a gospel sign of contradiction. Perhaps after all it is the celibates who have most to teach us about love. It is the deaf who are most sensitive to the line of melody — the music of the spheres. And it is the blind who really experience the dazzling power of colour and light. Go to where the pain is, and by God's grace you will find the pearl.

Saving Reconciliation

When Joseph's brothers saw that their father was dead, they said, 'It may be that Joseph will hate us and pay us back for all the evil which we did to him.' So they sent a message to Joseph, saying, 'Your father gave this command before he died, "Say to Joseph, Forgive, I pray you, the transgression of your brothers and their sin, because they did evil to you." And now, we pray you, forgive the transgression of the servants of the God of your father.' Joseph wept when they spoke to him. His brothers also came and fell down before him, and said, 'Behold, we are your servants.' But Joseph said to them, 'Fear not, for am I in the place of God? As for you, you meant evil against me; but God meant it for good, to bring it about that many people should be kept alive, as they are today. So do not fear; I will provide for you and your little ones.' Thus he reassured them and comforted them.   Genesis 50:15—21

His-story   This is surely one of the great turn arounds of history! The logical straightforward response of Joseph on meeting his brothers after all these years would have been to get his own back in every sense. Instead he puts everything into reverse. In the place of hatred Joseph responds with love. Instead of rejection there is acceptance; instead of shouts of anger there are tears of forgiveness.

And then we see perhaps one of the most exciting texts in the whole of the scriptures: 'You meant evil against me,' says Joseph to his brothers, 'but God meant it for good.'

Wherever there is repentance and forgiveness even what is bad can be used for good ends. God is after all the Lord of history precisely because he can bring good even out of evil. He always has the last word. In fact what emerges is something even more wonderful than the state of things before the evil was done. Forgiven mankind is even more highly esteemed than innocent mankind before the Fall. You cannot put the clock back and pretend it did not happen: you should not really in the end want to do that. However far down you went, forgiveness will always restore you even higher than you were before. This argument is so powerful that Paul has to check himself: 'Are we to continue in sin that grace may abound? By no means!' (Romans 6:1—2). We must always try of course, before the event, to reject evil and sin. But when we have sinned, if we will, in the name of God, ask for forgiveness then we should know that the God of the Bible can turn the evil and redeem it, raising us again to a newer and higher life. We call that life holiness and we rightly recognize such people as forgiven sinners by calling them saints. It is the saints who glorify God, for the good news which he has raised up is the new headline. It caps all the bad news of history. So *through* the sin of his brothers and *through* Joseph's forgiveness 'many people' are saved. Joseph is here both priest and victim — a true salvation figure.

The Jesus story 'You have heard that it was said, "An eye for an eye and a tooth for a tooth." But I say to you. . .' (Matthew 5:38—39). To repay our enemies in kind is to keep going down the same old road. It is a dead end. The most radical and revolutionary break with the disastrous and recurring story of family life, national life and indeed life in general is to reverse all that story which is written in blood across the pages of so much of our history — personal and national. Let evil stop with me and put love in where only hatred existed before. So Jesus teaches us to love our enemies and to pray for those who despitefully use us. He taught us to do that and so have many philosophers before. The difference is that Jesus did not only teach us to do it: he did it in his own life. 'Father forgive them for they know not what they do,' was his prayer as they were actually knocking in the nails. At that point history is reversed — he made history. No, rather Joseph did that. Jesus remade history.

My story So St Paul is right when he tells us that 'all things work together for good for those who love God' (Romans 8:28). Yes, all things, even our sins and weaknesses. Joseph's ironic question to his brothers is the mandate for the baptized Christian. 'Am I in the place of God?' Yes, in some wonderful way we are baptized to be Jesus Christ for others. As members of the Body of Christ, God can use us in his plan for the salvation 'of many'.

And all this because of the forgiveness of sins. 'I believe in the resurrection of the body and the forgiveness of sins.' They belong together. No wonder Augustine can cry, '*O felix culpa*' — O happy sin! It's enough to make you cry! Joseph did; so did Jesus.

JONAH:
THE RELUCTANT MISSIONARY

ONE thing is certain about the book of Jonah: we do not know when it was written. Scholars disagree about its dating and place it anywhere (for varying reasons) between the eighth and second centuries BC. That is a happy controversy, for in a real sense the story of Jonah is timeless. Like so much in the scriptures it is not so much the record of what happened, but rather of what happens and is continuing to happen throughout history.

There is one other reference in the Old Testament to a prophet called Jonah. He is associated with the court of Jeroboam II of Israel in the late eighth century. However, most scholars do not seriously identify the book of Jonah with that particular prophet. It is nevertheless interesting to note that the late eighth-century Jonah was from Gath-hepher, a little town very near Nazareth. Since Jonah is the only Old Testament minor prophet explicitly mentioned by Jesus in the New Testament and since Jesus closely identifies himself with the "three days" that Jonah spent in the belly of the whale, it is important to draw out the real significance of the story of Jonah and not to be side-tracked into unresolvable discussions about the date of the book.

Jonah means 'dove' and as such he is clearly a symbol of Israel. The background to the book and its message are clear. The Israel of Jonah's day was smug, exclusive and isolationist. Jonah is depicted as not caring for the city of Nineveh, its people or for its repentance. The ultimate message of the scriptures, and indeed of the gospel, is clear. It is put most succinctly in the mouths of those who heard Peter's declaration for the Gentiles: 'Then to the Gentiles also God has granted repentance unto life' (Acts 11:18). God loves the *whole* world and Jesus Christ died for *all*. The vocation of God's people in both the Old and New Testament is the same — 'to be a light to lighten the Gentiles'. So people are not called for privilege but for service. The Holy Spirit (the dove) is not given, neither are Christians anointed, for a personal spiritual massage. Rather they are to be sent — expelled — for mission with the message of God's great love for all on their lips and in their hearts.

In spite of himself, Jonah is called to be a salvation figure. Even in his resistance to the love of God, he witnesses to the power of that love which 'will not let me go'. If we reject or resist God's love for us it does not go away. 'It hurts to kick against the goads', St Paul is told. If we do, then that love which is intended to raise us up will have the same power to cast us down. Jonah is indeed J-shaped. Cast into the depths by his own resistance to God, he is raised up at the last and enabled to see the redemption of the outside world in the perspective of God's great love for the whole world.

Mission begins then in the heart of God himself. 'God so loved the world that he sent. . .' Since the dawn of time God has been *sending* his servants to the most uninspiring places, to the most unprepossessing people with the most impossible message! In these 'last days' he has sent his Son. Put another way we must say, 'Love is always ready to go out of its way'. Such is the nature of God's love for us: mission originates in the heart of God himself and all who are anointed in baptism with his love and spirit are automatically appointed to be heralds and missionaries to the nations of the world — beginning at Jerusalem, 'and in all Judea and Samaria and to the end of the earth' (Acts 1:8). Yes, even to Nineveh, 'that great city in which there are more than a hundred and twenty thousand persons who do not know their right hand from their left, and also much cattle'.

Questions for Discussion and Reflection

1. In what ways do we divide our lives between our 'church life' and the rest of life? Is there a line to be drawn between sacred and secular?

2. In what sense are Christians 'born again' and in what ways should Christians expect to 'die' daily?

3. In what ways have I experienced the power of God's Word at work in my life?

In the Way or on the Way?

> Now the word of the Lord came to Jonah the son of Amittai, saying, 'Arise, go to Nineveh, that great city, and cry against it; for their wickedness has come up before me.' But Jonah rose to flee to Tarshish from the presence of the Lord. He went down to Joppa and found a ship going to Tarshish; so he paid the fare, and went on board, to go with them to Tarshish, away from the presence of the Lord.
>
> But the Lord hurled a great wind upon the sea, and there was a mighty tempest on the sea, so that the ship threatened to break up. Then the mariners were afraid, and each cried to his god; and they threw the wares that were in the ship into the sea, to lighten it for them. But Jonah had gone down into the inner part of the ship and had lain down, and was fast asleep.   Jonah 1:1−5

His-story   Jonah is the reluctant missionary in the Old Testament. He is asked, like all missionaries, to go to the last place on earth he would ever have chosen to go and to love and serve the last sort of people on earth he would ever choose to serve! Yet the Lord was quite explicit, for 'in his hand are *all* the corners of the earth' (Psalm 95).

The good news of God's love, like all love, demands that we go out of our way to share that love with others. So we need to be followers on the way, going where we are sent and blown by the wind of the Spirit of mission. For if we are not on his way, for his ends, then we shall end up by always trying to have our way.

When the ship was not taking Jonah in the direction of God's mission, it experienced the wrath of God — a great storm — to the point where it seemed that the ship would break up. Jonah is nowhere to be found. He is trying to hide from God, of course. Of course he could not.

The Jesus story   The ship of the church — the Body of Christ — like Jesus in the New Testament, is anointed for mission. Jesus at his baptism was given the Holy Spirit and 'immediately' (as we are told in St Mark's gospel) Jesus was 'expelled' into the desert. The word in Greek is a powerful one, giving us the root in fact for nothing less than a 'ballistic' missile! He is expelled then into the most unprepossessing place of all for confrontation with evil in order to proclaim God's word. (Three times Jesus says: 'It is written. . . it is written. . . it is written. . .')

The ship of the church is intended for mission to the Gentiles — the outcasts. It is interesting that Jonah's ship went from Joppa. For it was at Joppa that St Peter had his blinding vision of the universal mission of the church. 'Truly I perceive,' says Peter as he interprets his dream at Joppa, 'that God shows no partiality, but in *every* nation any one who fears him and does what is right is acceptable to him' (Acts 10: 34—35). Every nation — even including the city of Nineveh: anyone, even the Gentiles! God shows no partiality. Jonah did. Do we?

My story The church will break up unless it is going where the Spirit of mission blows it. The church that lives to itself dies by itself. The gift of the Spirit is given to be given away. All the gifts of the Spirit are given for the sake of the whole Body. And that Body is given for the life of the world. The word of the Lord comes to us and is given to us as to Jonah, in order that we may take it to the ends of the earth.

So often we write off our everyday lives as secular and draw lines between the sphere of God and our secular life. We can be like Jonah if we take God's word and do not release it into the 'Ninevehs' of our lives. That may not be 'in distance' very far away from where we are standing. It is probably on our very doorstep: the rubbish collector in our streets; or the profession and work to which we have been called; the very place where we earn our living. It is easy to be a lay-reader, robed and in the sanctuary reading the word of God on a Sunday morning. God is calling us to proclaim and to *carry that word* of his assurance, which was given to us at our baptism, *dressed in our working clothes* from Monday to Friday and not simply on Sundays. That is our Nineveh. God cares in every corner of the earth. Do we?

Hide and Seek

And they said to one another, 'Come, let us cast lots, that we may know on whose account this evil has come upon us.' So they cast lots, and the lot fell upon Jonah. Then they said to him, 'Tell us, on whose account this evil has come upon us? What is your occupation? And whence do you come? What is your country? And of what people are you?' And he said to them, 'I am a Hebrew; and I fear the Lord, the God of heaven, who made the sea and the dry land.' Then the men were exceedingly afraid, and said to him, 'What is this that you have done!' For the men knew that he was fleeing from the presence of the Lord, because he had told them.   Jonah 1:7—10

His-story   Jonah was fleeing from the Lord. The psalmist in the Old Testament knew from experience how impossible it is to flee from God.

'Whither shall I go from thy Spirit?
Or whither shall I flee from thy presence?
If I ascend to heaven, thou art there!
If I make my bed in Sheol, thou art there!
If I take the wings of the morning
and dwell in the uttermost parts of the sea,
even there thy hand shall lead me,
and thy right hand shall hold me.'
                    (Psalm 139:7—10)

Poor old Jonah! But at least he had got things the right way round. He did not pretend that he was looking for God and that God was hiding from him. In the game of 'hide and seek' which most of us spend most of our time playing, again the psalmist is quite clear and gets it right: 'O Lord, thou hast searched me out and known me' (Psalm 139:1). God is doing the searching and we are running away from him into hiding. It all began when it all began: Adam said, 'I was afraid. . . and I hid myself' (Genesis 3:10). Ever since, fear has led all of us to cover up.

But God does not go off into a corner and sulk. His love sends him to the ends of the earth, 'to seek and to save' (Luke 19:10). Yet heaven is the place where God is and where his love is accepted and his name freely praised. Heaven is a question of attitude before it is a question of altitude. Hell has one similarity with heaven: it is also where God is present — and where we reject his presence and blaspheme his name. So in the Old

Testament, when the Philistines captured the ark of God and took it to Ashod and put it in the house of Dagon their god, the next morning their god was mutilated. Wherever they took the ark, the people experienced tumours. Finally in Ekron, there was a revolt and the people cried out, 'Send away the ark of the God of Israel, and let it return to its own place' (1 Samuel 5:11).

The Jesus story Not everyone was at home with Jesus in the New Testament. Demons cried out against him and were distinctly uncomfortable in his presence. The nice and sensible men of Gadara asked him (very politely of course) to leave their town after his presence had healed the demoniac and upset all their social structures. In the temple of God, where wrong attitudes prevailed, there was a confrontation. Yet God so loved the world that he sent his only Son into the world to save the world. Jesus presumably seldom felt at home in our world except where right attitudes prevailed and then for a moment it was like heaven on earth!

My story 'Mankind cannot bear very much reality' (T. S. Eliot). 'We are placed on this earth for a little while to learn to bear the beams of love' (William Blake). The 'hound of heaven' has been pursuing me since the moment God conceived of me. C. S. Lewis sharply reminds us that it is about as foolish to speak of a man looking for God as it is to speak of a mouse looking for a cat. It is always the other way around — the cat is looking for the mouse and the mouse had better look out! So when we are tempted to say rather blandly, 'Won't it be heavenly in heaven?', the answer is that it all depends on your attitude. It might be sheer hell if we are still running away from God himself — a kind of cosmic claustrophobia.

After all we are temples of the Holy Spirit. We only find the peace of heaven *within* when our spirit is uniting with his Spirit to cry 'Abba, Father'. Then we are in the right place, at the right time, glad to be there and with the right attitude. That is heaven — and of course by his grace it can be anywhere on earth or in eternity. The opposite is sheer hell — and that is where Jonah was — down in the bottom of the ship. Surely I have been there many times. Though again altitude is not the prime concern, but rather attitude. Jonah's attitude was all wrong and out of joint. Not unnaturally the sailors were quick to spot it. People generally are.

Downcast

So they took up Jonah and threw him into the sea; and the sea ceased from its raging. . . And the Lord appointed a great fish to swallow up Jonah; and Jonah was in the belly of the fish three days and three nights.

Then Jonah prayed to the Lord his God from the belly of the fish, saying,

'I called to the Lord, out of my distress, and he answered me; out of the belly of Sheol I cried, and thou didst hear my voice. For thou didst cast me into the deep, into the heart of the seas, and the flood was round about me; all thy waves and thy billows passed over me. Then I said, "I am cast out from thy presence; how shall I again look upon thy holy temple?" The waters closed in over me, the deep was round about me; weeds were wrapped about my head at the roots of the mountains. I went down to the land whose bars closed upon me for ever; yet thou didst bring up my life from the Pit, O Lord my God.'

Jonah 1:15, 17—2:6

His-story 'They took him up' and threw him down! When we are down, God raises us up! There is the contrast. It is easy to take people up (and causes of course) when they are prospering or when it is the thing to do! God truly loves us. He does not just take up our cause — poverty, abuse, alcoholism, homelessness, age-concern! He loves poor men and women; the children who are abused and know not love. He loves those who simply do not know how to face life without a 'drink in their hands'. He is not the champion of problems. He is the one who throughout the Old Testament 'rejoices with those who rejoice and weeps with those who weep'. He comes where we are in order to take us where we could not go by our own resources.

And so in the belly of the whale, when Jonah bottoms out, in the depths of despair, in words borrowed from the psalter and some words of worship from the temple of Israel, Jonah levels with God. Perhaps the best preparation for worship is depression! God's ancient people the Jews reached unsurpassed heights of praise, adoration and worship but, of all races, they have suffered brokenness perhaps almost more than any other race. Auschwitz strains our doctrine of man beyond credibility. It is hard to believe that twentieth-century, cultured, educated mankind could cast down other human beings so far. It is depravity beyond credibility. All

God's J-shaped people have at some point been thus downcast and outcast — beyond the pale.

The Jesus story So we should not be surprised if Jesus of Nazareth found no room in the inn. He said of himself, 'Foxes have holes, and birds of the air have nests; but the Son of man has nowhere to lay his head' (Matthew 8:20). He clearly identifies with Jonah and those three days in the belly of the whale. And then — the most alarming and disarming text of all is when we come to the point of it all: — 'My God, my God, why hast thou forsaken me?' (Mark 15:34). We find the echo of this text of course in the Psalms. The note was struck ultimately and forever on Calvary Hill. But then we find all the human story in the Psalms because God has identified with the human story and the human predicament. Before the time of Christ and since then, God's J-shaped people have been as low as that many times and in many places. Whether it is the dung hill of Job or the Calvary Hill of Jesus or the belly of the whale — we have to believe that such depths are possible within the contours of human experience. 'Praise to the Holiest in the height', says Cardinal Newman. But so do all the religions of the world. Perhaps only Judaism and Christianity can go on to say, 'and in the depths be praise'.

My story 'I am powerless over drink.' The first step on the road to recovery for alcoholics is to admit that they are powerless and then in that moment of 'powerlessness' to know what it is to be given strength. It is in my defeat that I can accept his victory; it is in my despair and death that I shall be given hope and new life. That is the shape of real life. We need to know the geography of true strength. All God's J-shaped people at some point have been *there*. (We call it the belly of the whale. We do not need to ask whether we can swallow the story of Jonah and the whale! We have to allow it the incredible capacity to swallow us.) At some point it all becomes too much. I am engulfed, overwhelmed and overtaken. The witness and story of all really J-shaped people is that at such moments I do not fall right through the black holes of the universe. Along with Jonah in the whale's belly — and with Jesus on Calvary Hill — at such points I can cry out, 'Into thy hands, O Lord, I commend my spirit.' It is then that I discover for myself the awesome contradiction that 'underneath are the everlasting arms'.

The Man from Down Under!

> . . . Jonah prayed to the Lord his God from the belly of the fish, saying. . . 'Deliverance belongs to the Lord!' And the Lord spoke to the fish, and it vomited out Jonah upon the dry land.
>
> Then the word of the Lord came to Jonah the second time, saying, 'Arise, go to Nineveh, that great city, and proclaim to it the message that I tell you.' So Jonah arose and went to Nineveh, according to the word of the Lord. Now Nineveh was an exceedingly great city, three days' journey in breadth. Jonah began to go into the city, going a day's journey. And he cried, 'Yet forty days, and Nineveh shall be overthrown!'
>
> Jonah 2:1, 9–3:4

My story In a profound theological and sacramental sense, Jonah was 'born again'. He was really no use to God nor man while he was his own man going where his own whim took him and driven by purely natural preferences. In a real sense he had to die and be born again — go down and be raised up. That was to be the shape of his life — his life story was essentially J-shaped throughout. When the sailors took him and threw him overboard, that was the end. Jonah was finished. Now God could begin. Jonah was both the same Jonah and a very different Jonah when his feet touched dry ground the other side of the trauma. By that time he had been through it — and a new life was beginning. The great fish was to all intents and purposes his tomb — but the tomb turned out to be a womb from which new life came forth. Jonah, like Jesus, was the man from down under!

The Jesus story 'How can a man be born when he is old?', asks the incredulous Nicodemus at the very beginning of St John's gospel. 'Can he enter a second time into his mother's womb and be born?' The straightforward answer must surely be — 'No'. Yet Jesus is not trying to introduce Nicodemus to revival nor encourage him to hope that he might come back to life. Jonah was one of the early people who came back to life. As such he belongs to the line of Lazarus. Poor old Lazarus: he did not rise from the dead, he only came back to life. What a pathetic prospect! Back to life — the same old life, poor old Lazarus — there is no good news there. No wonder Jesus wept!

For Jesus did not rise from the dead. He died in whatever sense we mean by using that word. He passed through life and was raised *through* death — the wall of partition between the God of life and this second-hand life we call life. Life cut off from God by sin and alienation is surely a living death. Yet Jesus delights to speak of Jonah's experience as a sign of the sort of passage, or exodus, that he is to accomplish in his death and resurrection. When Jesus spoke with Moses and Elijah on the mountain of Transfiguration about his forthcoming 'exodus', this distinction must surely have been high on his agenda (Luke 9:28—36). 'No, I shall not be just coming back to life—another one of those men from down under. That is in the tradition of such cases as Jonah in the belly of the great fish for three days and three nights. You cannot enter your mother's womb a second time and be born again just like that. You must be born again not only by water but by water and the Spirit and then you can be raised up through death to a new quality of life in direct life-giving communion with God.' Jesus was the first to do that. Jonah like Lazarus was only a prototype.

His-story   So at the end of the fourth gospel we see Nicodemus again for a brief moment. It is Good Friday evening. He is with Joseph of Aramathea making all the undertaker's arrangements. He is at the tomb. Once again it is night. But perhaps there was a sudden flash of lightning for there was certainly a moment of insight. 'In my end is my beginning.' Perhaps after all the tomb can be a womb and perhaps we need to die to live.

Truth to tell we have to 'die' many times. (Perhaps Jonah should be the patron saint of undertakers. After all he is one of the more lugubrious characters of the Old Testament and would wear his uniform quite well!)

Can we learn to live in that J-shaped way? 'Dying, behold we live' cries St Paul. That was his experience. Nothing could have looked more like a dead end than Damascus. Yet after all it turned out to be for him— a bit like Jonah when his feet had hit the dry ground — the beginning of a new life. But then the real life (like love) is always somewhat head-over-heels (*boule versé* as the French call it).

A Change of Direction

And the people of Nineveh believed God; they proclaimed a fast, and put on sackcloth, from the greatest of them to the least of them. Then tidings reached the king of Nineveh, and he arose from his throne, removed his robe, and covered himself with sackcloth, and sat in ashes. And he made proclamation and published through Nineveh, 'By the decree of the king and his nobles: Let neither man nor beast, herd nor flock, taste anything; let them not feed, or drink water, but let man and beast be covered with sackcloth, and let them cry mightily to God; yea, let every one turn from his evil way and from the violence which is in his hands. Who knows, God may yet repent and turn from his fierce anger, so that we perish not?'   Jonah 3:5—9

His-story Clearly the word which Jonah had preached was effective: it was a word of power. The people at Nineveh were moved. They repented — from the greatest of them to the least of them. Jonah, reluctant though he was, had obediently proclaimed the word of God. In the end he did what God told him to do. In his turn the king also proclaimed and the people did what *he* told them to do. The word of repentance can catch on and take fire.

All this has nothing whatever to do necessarily with eloquence, clever words or creating a great impression. The preacher of the scriptures has often not been especially eloquent. Moses could not string two words together, it would seem, yet he moved (literally) the whole people of Israel out of Egypt through the desert and to the threshold of the promised land. Although Aaron was technically the better speaker, it was Moses who really *moved* God's people.

And why? Because in the first place Moses had been moved by God's word — literally he was sent to Pharaoh. He was obedient to that word.

God's word is not ineffective. It does not return to him empty. We are told that the word of the Lord came a second time to Jonah. On second thoughts (repentance — *metanoia*), Jonah went where he was told to go and said what he was told to say. That word was a word of power.

The Jesus story In the New Testament Jesus is the Word of God sent to Nazareth. ('Can anything good come out of Nazareth?') It was the last place on earth (rather like Nineveh) that most of us would ever have chosen for the fountain of world mission.

Jesus, the Word of God, speaks not like the scribes and Pharisees — rather, he speaks as one having authority. His word literally carries weight. It takes a centurion within an authority structure, to spot that. When Jesus speaks, things happen. (It takes a man of authority — a centurion — to spot another 'centurion'.)

God's word is a word of power — but power not in the sense of imperial power ('*imperium*'). Jesus rejects that sort of power in his trial before Pilate. No: the power of the word of God lies in its authority ('*auctoritas*'). The word of God is a mover and a shaker!

In the fourth gospel Jesus sees himself very much as one under authority, living in total obedience to the Father. He only accomplishes (effectively) what the Father tells him to do and says what the Father tells him to say. He has no authority of his own. Authority is in an exact ratio to obedience. Jonah would never have been an effective preacher unless eventually (however reluctantly) he had gone where God told him to go and said what God had told him to say.

My story Mary says to the servants at Cana of Galilee, — 'Do whatever he tells you' (John 2:5). She should know, for she was obedient to that word of God when it was brought to her by the angel in the first place. She was the first human being by grace to say an unqualified 'Yes' to God's word — Amen: Let it be to me. So in Bethlehem and in Cana of Galilee there is a miracle and the totally unexpected happens, for '*with* God nothing will be impossible' (Luke 1:37).

The church will only speak with true authority to the extent that it is faithful and obedient to God's word. That word can move heaven and earth, mountains and even the king and people of Nineveh. For although 'heaven and earth shall pass away' God's word shall not pass away. Amen. Alleluya!

Anger or Agony?

When God saw what they did, how they turned from their evil way, God repented of the evil which he had said he would do to them; and he did not do it.

But it displeased Jonah exceedingly, and he was angry. And he prayed to the Lord and said, 'I pray thee, Lord, is not this what I said when I was yet in my country? That is why I made haste to flee to Tarshish; for I knew that thou art a gracious God and merciful, slow to anger, and abounding in steadfast love, and repentest of evil. Therefore now, O Lord, take my life from me, I beseech thee, for it is better for me to die than to live.' And the Lord said, 'Do you do well to be angry?' Then Jonah went out of the city and sat to the east of the city, and made a booth for himself there. He sat under it in the shade, till he should see what would become of the city.   Jonah 3:10—4:5

His-story   'Do you do well to be angry?' We have all sat where Jonah sat! Can you see him? He wanted above all else to indulge that ghastly phrase: 'There, I told you so!' It is a frightfully self-righteous phrase. It is always on the lips of those who want to play God.

God repented! It means in crude language that he had second thoughts. 'For the love of God is broader than the measures of man's mind,' says F. W. Faber, the nineteenth-century hymn-writer. The God of the Old Testament is a God of passion and therefore the God of compassion. He meets us more than half-way — because he is more than ready to go out of his way. Of course Jonah would have preferred to stay just where he was. The last thing in the world he — and people like him — wanted to do was to get all involved with this Nineveh 'business' — or any other business — in anything other than his own business. He just wanted to be proved right! He had taken up a cause.

The God of the Old Testament is different from all of that. He is distinctively different from the ancient gods of the Pantheon. He is pathetically — literally — partial to some people because he wants in the end to be gracious to all people. He loves the people of Nineveh — down to the last old cow (Jonah 4:11)! Jonah's failing was not that he went too far. He was not ready to consider even going far enough. He did not begin to care — really to care for the people of Nineveh.

So we see him sitting there watching the city complacently, wearing his steel-rimmed spectacles. Mankind is at its most sinful not so much when it cares too much but rather when it does not care enough. The gods of the Pantheon were without passion — apathetic, if you like — detached, out of touch and untouchable. They presided over the world from a safe distance, untouched by the pains and passions of our world in all of its confusions. They would always want the last word — and it would always be the same — 'There, I told you so! What else can you expect from such people?' Jonah is in that league. The God of the Old Testament — and the New, as we shall see — is most certainly not — thank God! *He* repented. He was clearly moved by the people of Nineveh. The God of the Bible has second thoughts. Jonah did not think the people of Nineveh were even worth second thoughts. He wanted to play God — the old-fashioned kind.

The Jesus story '(Jonah) sat under it' (a booth which he had made for himself) — he just sat there, 'till he should see what would become of the city.' Jesus in the New Testament 'wept over' the city of Jerusalem. The very opposite to what we might expect. The God whom we are coming to know in Jesus Christ does not preside indifferently over the tragedy of our world. He does not sit on a throne so much as he hangs on a tree. In the garden of Gethsemane the ancient god-like figure of the ancient world would have stood upright, unmoved and immovable. He would have remained alone staring his fate coldly and bravely in the face. But no! Not a bit of it. Jesus takes his three closest friends and asks them to stay very close to him. With blood, sweat and tears he enters into the agony of his Passion. 'You stay here, while I go just over there and sweat it out.' There is nothing untouchable about this God of ours. We do not have a high priest 'untouched' or untouchable ('unable to sympathize with our weaknesses' Hebrews 4:15). As Jonah sat outside the city of Nineveh untouched and untouchable — waiting to be proved right — he could not have been more ungodly. God help him!

My story We live in a strange world of inverted religious snobbery. For it is not true that if we cease to accept the judgement of God we become accepting. The very opposite is true. We become *selectively* judgemental, indifferent and self-righteous. We make a religion of our own as surely as Jonah made a booth for himself, and we shelter under it — safely detached from the agonies of the world and always in the right. By the end, Jonah did not feel even angry — or any real agony of any sort. In the end he felt nothing. Jonah was seriously in danger of ultimate damnation — to be unmoved and immovable — apathetic and truly pathetic. Come off it, Jonah, for God's sake!

Paranoia or Metanoia?

> And the Lord God appointed a plant, and made it come up over Jonah, that it might be a shade over his head, to save him from his discomfort. So Jonah was exceedingly glad because of the plant. But when dawn came up the next day, God appointed a worm which attacked the plant, so that it withered. When the sun rose, God appointed a sultry east wind, and the sun beat upon the head of Jonah so that he was faint; and he asked that he might die, and said, 'It is better for me to die than to live.' But God said to Jonah, 'Do you do well to be angry for the plant?' And he said, 'I do well to be angry, angry enough to die.' And the Lord said, 'You pity the plant, for which you did not labour, nor did you make it grow, which came into being in a night, and perished in a night. And should not I pity Nineveh, that great city, in which there are more than a hundred and twenty thousand persons who do not know their right hand from their left, and also much cattle?'   Jonah 4:6—11

His-story 'Angry enough to die?' Yet God is even in our anger! 'God appointed a plant. . . that it might be a shade' over (Jonah's) head, to save him from his own self-inflicted discomfort. What an incredibly gracious and generous God we worship! He did not have to do it. There are no laws in the universe to protect people from their own self-inflicted, self-destruction!

At last, however, Jonah begins to change his outlook. It is not all bad news after all. 'He was exceedingly glad because of the plant.' The world is not totally against him after all! History can appear as though life were against us. The story of Israel is not a happy story. Yet the opposite is equally, if not more true, for we can end up if we are not careful against life. 'This day,' says the Lord, 'I have set before you (the way of) life and (the way of) death. . . therefore choose life' (Deuteronomy 30:19).

Jonah had to learn to see things and life in a totally new perspective. God showed him a new scale of values. Jonah was pleased because a plant gave him shelter and protected him from the heat. He cherished the plant — a created thing. Yet plants come and go. All people are made in the image of God. We are called to love our neighbour because God created him or her. The image of God is right there, and sitting next to you.

The Jesus story The call of Jesus in the New Testament is a call to repentance — a call to see things in a new light. Jesus challenges people to a new scale of values. 'If God so clothes the grass which is alive in the field today and tomorrow is thrown into the oven, how much more will he clothe you, O men of little faith!' (Luke 12:28). Jesus shed his blood for everybody — Greek or Jew, black or white. We cannot over-estimate our worth to God. The danger is that we shall under-estimate others' worth — the people of Nineveh. We write people off as just ordinary. There is no such person in this world as an ordinary person!

My story In the end there are only two alternatives: paranoia or metanoia. Paranoia tempts me to think that life is against me, or just reduces me to an attitude which is against life. Jonah had driven himself into paranoia. God was calling him to metanoia — repentance — to take a second look at Nineveh and see it in a new light. Perhaps we ought not so much to try to change the world. The first thing we have to do is much more difficult. It starts with us. We need to change our attitude to the world. That is much more revolutionary and radical. We project on to the world our own inner attitudes. Perhaps Jonah could not begin to love Nineveh because he did not value himself. God first showed him that he loved him, by sheltering him from the heat. 'We love because he first loved us.' God showed love and concern for Jonah and hopefully that would change Jonah's attitude even to Nineveh.

A missionary is not someone who sets out to love the world. He or she is someone who has first discovered the awesome secret that they are loved and lovable. Then and then only in the place of paranoia we find metanoia. We simply have to share that secret. We are not here first to do good but to discover that 'the Lord has promised good to me'. That turns everything upside down.

JOB: THE PATIENT

JOB was not an Israelite, but a resident of the land of Uz, which may possibly have been located in the north-east of Palestine. It is doubtful that this book purports to be mainly historical in its thrust. It clearly rises to a high calibre of poetry and as such is the first of five poetical books in the Old Testament.

Once again we are concerned here not so much with an historical event which may have happened, yet we are powerfully struck with the realism of the story: surely, this is precisely what happens all the time! The wicked prosper; the good and the innocent suffer. 'It never rains but it pours!' is an apt commentary on the list of catastrophies which happened like 'one damned thing after another' to Job's family and eventually to Job himself in the two opening chapters of the book. Yet if this is so we are driven to ask a fundamental question: Where are we to find justice in this universe in which the good suffer, or to use the words of Jesus (Matthew 5:45), in which God 'sends rain on the just and on the unjust'? Where and when is unrighteousness to be dealt with? Clearly suffering has been a real stumbling-block to belief in God since the dawn of time and every serious religion has had to try to tackle this fundamental theological problem.

The book of Job makes a significant and important contribution to this ongoing theological and psychological debate. While the book of Job does not come up with any slick and easy answers, it makes some really important contributions to the discussion — a discussion which will not end until the end of history.

The following points are made in the book of Job:

1.   The problem of suffering does not originate in history but rather invades history from outside of history. Suffering is a cosmic problem with its roots in eternity (that discussion between God and Satan in the early chapters). As P. T. Forsyth wrote, 'There was a Calvary above which is the mother of it all'.

2.   God does not reward — nor possibly bribe conduct by promising rewards. At least, not in this life. A mature choice for Yahweh must be based on faith and trust even in the face of adversity.

3.   Plausible answers to suffering such as those put forward by Job's so-called comforters are an abomination to God.

4.   Suffering takes us to the very heart of God himself. There is no answer which can make sense of the problem of suffering in merely intellectual terms. Suffering is bound up in some mysterious way with the very nature of God and can only be approached as a mystery. Mystery however, in this sense, does not mean that which denies exploration but rather that which is not

exhausted by all our explorations. In so far as the infinite creator is unknowable by the finite mind of the creature, so to that extent the answer to suffering is beyond all our knowledge (cp. the words of the Lord from the whirlwind in chapters 38 to 41).

5.   Trust and faith in and through suffering are founded upon the conviction that although the equation cannot be squared and resolved *in* history, it demands something of a courtroom vindication after life and beyond history — 'at the last day'. Then God will be the advocate for those who have suffered and kept faith. The acceptance of death can itself be that ultimate act of faith and trust.

6.   The theme of innocent suffering is always below the surface in the Old Testament. It is Jesus who brings it out into the open in his own Passion, suffering and death. It is in fellowship with him and his sufferings that Christians can find hope and justice in an otherwise hopeless and unjust world. Yet their discovery is not in the form of an intellectually satisfying answer to the problem, but rather in the experience of self-transcendance. As the psalmist said, 'I could not understand this until I went into the sanctuary of God' (Psalm 73:16—17); or in Job's own words at the climax of the book, 'I had heard of thee by the hearing of the ear, but now my eye sees thee; therefore I despise myself, and repent in dust and ashes' (Job 42:5—6).

Job is truly J-shaped. In the last chapter Yahweh restores Job's fortunes. It has to be admitted that this is not usually the case. It is only in life beyond life that Job and Jesus are raised up in the resurrection to eternal life. In this sense the book of Job begins to bang loud and hard on that door which demands life *after* death and beyond death, in which the righteousness of faith and trust is finally vindicated and upheld.

Questions for Discussion and Reflection

1.   What does it mean to be 'a good patient'?

2.   Where have I experienced break*down* in order to break *through* in my own life, or in the lives of others?

3.   In what ways do we come to know God? What are the dangers in claiming to know God?

─── Right End of the Stick ───

There was a man in the land of Uz, whose name was Job; and that man was blameless and upright, one who feared God, and turned away from evil. . . Now there was a day when the sons of God came to present themselves before the Lord, and Satan also came among them. . . And the Lord said to Satan, 'Have you considered my servant Job, that there is none like him on the earth, a blameless and upright man, who fears God and turns away from evil?' Then Satan answered the Lord, 'Does Job fear God for nought? Hast thou not put a hedge about him and his house and all that he has, on every side? Thou hast blessed the work of his hands, and his possessions have increased in the land. But put forth thy hand now, and touch all that he has, and he will curse thee to thy face.' And the Lord said to Satan, 'Behold, all that he has is in your power; only upon himself do not put forth your hand.' So Satan went forth from the presence of the Lord.   Job 1:1, 6, 8−12

His-story Like all great stories, the story of Job appears more than once on the landscape of human story-telling, in different locations and in different languages. Yet it is precisely because a similar story occurs in more places than one that its appeal is universal. Its roots go deeper than mere history and its echoes resonate beyond time. Such stories are true because they are clearly true, not simply because they happen also to appear in the scriptures.

So we find a Job who is not peculiar to Judaism in Mohammedan legend, where he vows to give his wife something like a hundred stripes when he finally recovers his health. Happily for her, Allah insists that Job should give her only one blow from a palm branch with a hundred leaves on it! The scene of the book of Job is set possibly in remote Arabia in something of a caricature period of the ancient patriarchs. Clearly there was a figure of legend and myth (they can sometimes fuse together) in the literature of the ancient world. Yet the language and philosophy and theology of the book of Job are of a much later period. We must not 'mistake the general antiquity of the picture of Job for evidence of a date equally remote; as a matter of fact it would have been as inconceivable a product of Israel's life in that remote age as would be Tennyson's *In Memoriam* in the times of the early Britons' (H. Wheeler Robinson, *The Cross in the Old Testament*).

The Jesus story Job haunts the scriptures throughout as a legendary figure of righteousness and suffering. Ezekiel sees him along with Noah and Daniel as deliverance and salvation figures and as men of outstanding righteousness. The epistle of James in the New Testament points to Job as a figure well known for endurance and steadfastness (5:11). Common parlance still speaks today of the patience of Job.

For truth to tell you do not have to go very far or very deep before you collide with the stumbling-block of apparently undeserved suffering. So in Mark's gospel three times, 'like claps of thunder', Jesus warns his disciples of the necessity of suffering as part of the path to glory (8:31−38, 9:30−32, 10:32−34). He began to teach this theme according to St Mark's gospel immediately after Peter's confession of faith at Caesarea Philippi. Peter simply could not accept the teaching. In turn Jesus rebukes Peter and actually calls him Satan accusing him of thinking only 'as men think and not as God thinks' (Mark 8:33).

My story A large advertisement for good brakes by the highway in America reads: 'Stop sliding through life!' In fact you cannot just slide through real life. There are all kinds of 'braking' points. The road to glory and ultimate communion with God passes right *through* the pain and darkness of the world. You will find Job in every seam of literature and life and the deeper you dig the more persistently you will come across him. He does not answer many of the real questions; he leaves most of that to his unfortunate and somewhat superficial friends. You cannot make suffering (least of all apparently undeserved suffering) a matter for debate. It is essentially a mystery. More than that, there is a fellowship in suffering and Job is a mysterious, shadowy member on the edge of that group with Jesus and his cross sharply in relief at the centre. For, we need to notice that the book of Job is ignorant of the cosmic origins of his suffering. We share in that same ignorance and that is surely what makes the problem so very painful.

We need to see all this from the perspective of God and unlike St Peter we shall then begin to think not as the world thinks but rather from the divine perspective of Calvary Hill, where light and darkness, glory and death converge. Furthermore, we shall not be in danger of seeing glory as the same as success, nor death as the ultimate defeat, but rather as the ultimate act of faith vindicated in the resurrection. All this is not the solution to a problem, but rather a different way entirely of putting the question. Perhaps St Peter never really saw it that way until, as tradition insists, he asked to be crucified upside down in order that he might enter that fellowship of suffering along with Job and Jesus and all the other J-shaped people, who are beginning to see things the right way up!

For God's Sake!

Now there was a day when (Job's) sons and daughters were eating and drinking wine in their eldest brother's house; and there came a messenger to Job, and said, 'The oxen were ploughing and the asses feeding beside them; and the Sabeans fell upon them and took them, and slew the servants with the edge of the sword; and I alone have escaped to tell you.' While he was yet speaking, there came another, and said, 'The fire of God fell from heaven and burned up the sheep and the servants, and consumed them; and I alone have escaped to tell you.' While he was yet speaking, there came another, and said. . . 'Your sons and daughters were eating and drinking wine in their eldest brother's house; and behold, a great wind came across the wilderness, and struck the four corners of the house, and it fell upon the young people, and they are dead; and I alone have escaped to tell you.'

Then Job arose, and rent his robe, and shaved his head, and fell upon the ground, and worshipped. And he said, 'Naked I came from my mother's womb, and naked shall I return; the Lord gave, and the Lord has taken away; blessed be the name of the Lord.'

In all this Job did not sin or charge God with wrong.   Job 1:13−22

His-story   And so we watch Job's world being broken apart. The ring of truth here is alarmingly clear and authentic. For when it starts happening it all seems to happen at once, so that we are led to say, 'It couldn't have come at a worse time!' He lost family and wealth in a single day. Yet notice Job's response and the reason why in this part of his suffering he was sinless. In his agony he yet recognized his wealth and his family for what they were — namely, gifts from God. Of course it is superhuman almost inhuman to come to such a statement in one step and in one breath. 'Naked I came from my mother's womb, and naked shall I return; the Lord gave, and the Lord has taken away; blessed be the name of the Lord.' Clearly here is a deeply religious man who is free from the idolatry of family and wealth. Very terrible though his lot is, it is not the end of his world. He has not mistaken the creation for the Creator, the gifts for the Giver. In all that therefore, 'he did not sin' — he did not miss the point of life, which is to enjoy to the full and to share to the full all the most beautiful things and people of life, yet to know in the end that they are indeed all gifts, graciously given to us by a generous Giver.

The Jesus story Again and again in the gospel Jesus cautions his disciples against idolatry. The Golden Calf of the Old Testament takes many forms — family, friends, beauty, money, success. He tries to show us how to handle such gifts in such a way that we can keep them for ever. The teaching is consistently J-shaped throughout. What I try to possess and make my own I shall lose. Yet by contradiction what I am willing and ready to release I shall keep forever. In the first case, however rich I may be, I shall end up by being a rather poor old thing if I belong to my possessions and end up possessed by my possessions. In the latter case, however poor I may be (especially in wordly goods), at the end of the day I shall know myself to be richly endowed for eternity.

My story Job's first response to the bad news was worship: the same worship of the same God as if the news had been good. That is true worship. If we worship God only when things are going well (in the sunshine of life) and curse and blaspheme him in the bad times of tears, our worship is little better than manipulation, therapy or blackmail.

We worship the true God simply and only because he is God. And furthermore, he is God because he is *worth* more than any other object of our 'worthship'. It is in and through the bad times that we draw closer to God for his own sake — in the stillness and the darkness when all our passions are spent. It is then that we know that although there are many and priceless gifts which I have lost ('awhile' — Newman), there is still the ineffable Giver who may the better be able to give himself to me when all the other gifts are not there to get in the way so much.

None of this explains or justifies suffering. None of this should lead us to that most dangerous and misguided phrase, 'This has been sent to try us'. Like Job we are ignorant also of the ultimate source or origin of suffering. On this earth we always shall be. Yet in Jesus we see not an answer but rather a process. On Calvary Hill and in his sufferings, our humanity is drawn closer to God the Father than at any other point in history or on earth. . . with one possible exception: when Job was on his dunghill with head shaved. 'We shall, before we have done, know that there is more than one spiritual tie which links Job on his dunghill with Christ in Gethsemane' (H. Wheeler Robinson).

What Sort of God?

And the Lord said to Satan, 'Have you considered my servant Job, that there is none like him on the earth, a blameless and upright man, who fears God and turns away from evil? He still holds fast his integrity, although you moved me against him, to destroy him without cause.' Then Satan answered the Lord, 'Skin for skin! All that a man has he will give for his life. But put forth thy hand now, and touch his bone and his flesh, and he will curse thee to thy face.' And the Lord said to Satan, 'Behold, he is in your power; only spare his life.'

So Satan went forth from the presence of the Lord, and afflicted Job with loathsome sores from the sole of his foot to the crown of his head. And he took a potsherd with which to scrape himself, and sat among the ashes. Then his wife said to him, 'Do you still hold fast your integrity? Curse God, and die.' But he said to her, 'You speak as one of the foolish women would speak. Shall we receive good at the hand of God, and shall we not receive evil?' In all this Job did not sin with his lips.   Job 2:3−10

His-story 'Away from the dwelling place of men, (Job) lies on the burnt dungheaps which are a familiar feature of the neighbourhood of oriental villages. There we must picture him. . . thither comes his wife, with her so natural outburst, womanly in the depths of her sympathy to the sufferer, angry with God because of her love for Job' (H. Wheeler Robinson).

Yet from that position (and at some point we have all been to that place in our own hearts) we are in no position either to know the first word of this whole drama nor the last. The first word is before and outside of history, as we have seen. Job, his wife and his countless 'comforters' down the ages (BC) could only speculate about the first words of the creation drama. We do not know all that was involved in the divine pregnancy. It is easy to believe in God and that there is a god who created. The difficulty still remains: 'Yes, but what sort of a god?' The innocent, unjust and undeserved suffering of the world tempts us to talk like Job's wife. If we argue for the existence of the Creator from the state of his creation (the argument from design, as we say) then such a god is either incompetent, indifferent or some sort of vivisectionist (to quote C. S. Lewis in his despair). So why not curse such a god? He may not even hear us, let alone care.

The Jesus story Jesus is the first word and God's last word to us. We do not have to speculate even like the author of the book of Job and try to have one ear on the heavenly dialogue between the scenes. By word and by deed Jesus shows us a God who cares, who loves, who creates and who in some mysterious way is himself at the very heart of suffering. Therefore to get to the heart of the matter is inevitably at some point to touch base with suffering, and so to be drawn closer to God in Christ.

History is a process arising out of a word (the Word). Furthermore that word is love. Love must create: infinite love must create infinitely. History is a birth process — the whole creation 'groaning' and 'travailing', *waiting* (Romans 8:22) — thus, the *patience* of Job. There is the frustration of evil in all of that process (which is possibly the principal cause of pain), but we do 'not receive evil' from God.

'Inscribed upon the Cross we see
in shining letters, "God is love".'
(Thomas Kelly)

My story God's chosen people are chosen to have a special part in this patient process. While we can never know from Job's point of view the root cause of such suffering, we do know that it can have a purpose. Christians differ from other religions of the world at precisely this point. In Mohammedanism fatalism takes over and speaks of all suffering as 'the will of Allah' — Allah who displays power more than love. In Buddhism, there is an unwillingness to be realistic about suffering. 'In the midst of sorrow there is no Nirvana, and in Nirvana there is no sorrow.' Only Christianity of all world religions has a problem about suffering, because it insists that God cares.

Christianity has both a first and last word. 'God so loved the world that he sent' his son to save the world. And, 'God was in Christ reconciling the world to himself.' Job's story, the Jesus story and my story are mysteriously an essential turn in the plot of that whole drama which began in the heart of God (not just the courts of heaven). It will conclude (and perhaps make sense) only in the bosom of the Father, along with Job and Jesus and all his J-shaped friends. Suffering has its origins before history, and will only make ultimate sense beyond history — in other words, *in* Christ, the Alpha and Omega of love, creation and suffering.

Undergoing to Overcome

Then Job answered. . . 'All my intimate friends abhor me, and those whom I have loved have turned against me. My bones cleave to my skin and to my flesh, and I have escaped by the skin of my teeth. Have pity on me, have pity on me, O you my friends, for the hand of God has touched me! Why do you, like God, pursue me? Why are you not satisfied with my flesh?

'Oh that my words are written! Oh that they were inscribed in a book! Oh that with an iron pen and lead they were graven in the rock for ever! For I know that my Redeemer lives, and at last he will stand upon the earth; and after my skin has been thus destroyed, then without my flesh I shall see God, whom I shall see on my side, and my eyes shall behold, and not another. My heart faints within me!'

Job 19:1, 19—27

His-story   Job's three friends have visited him in his distress — Eliphaz the Temanite, Bildad the Shuhite and Zophar the Naamathite. They do not listen: they speak. They appear to believe they have good advice for Job which he needs to hear. They lecture him on his bad theology. In a word, they do all the wrong things when visiting a patient!

The names of the three friends and so-called comforters are interesting because their names mean different things. What the names stand for, however, are hardy annuals and you will find them in every language and in every culture under the sun. People are judgemental, sentimental, even detrimental in their attitude to suffering. There were all kinds of views around at the time when the book of Job was written; as there are today on this thorny question. In some sense they are always around, these comforters of Job.

The Jesus story   When in St John's gospel Jesus is asked about a blind man: 'Who sinned? This man or his parents?', his answer is unequivocal. 'Neither,' is his reply (John 9:3). He refutes one of the contemporary attitudes about ill-health, poverty and suffering: namely, that it is some kind of punishment by God; it was God's judgement upon the sinner. That is not the way God has chosen to deal with sin — by punishing the sinner. He has chosen a yet more excellent way. He himself has undergone the effects of sin (without sinning) and has overcome the effects of sin, while still *loving* the sinner. That is God's J-shaped response to sin: undergo in order to overcome. It is certainly not divine apathy or indifference, but rather in Christ it is supreme sympathy — to suffer with. By derivation Christ is the supreme patient, as well as the divine physician.

My story Christians are called to be neither judgemental nor sentimental about disease and suffering. We are called to be supremely realistic. On every front, politically, economically, medically and in every way we are called to fight suffering and disease and to push back its frontiers.

Yet individually as well as corporately, where this temporally fails and when we have done all that we can do (and always together with God through prayer), then there is a moment of turning.

We then turn to face the suffering and even to embrace it. We sympathize with the patient: we cease from words. We take hold of the hand of the patient — 'the hand of God has touched me' (Job 19:21). We seek to come alongside the patient in his or her passion. We can do this in the sure knowledge (which humanly speaking Job did not have) that God himself has already come alongside us in Christ and that by sympathy he has made our passion his own by undergoing all that we could ever be asked to undergo.

Christ, if you like, is the model patient. (The root is the same in Greek and Latin as the word patience, passion, apathy and sympathy: all these words are related and are in the same family — the family of J-shaped people.) The good patient in the hospital of the fellowship of the redeemed knows that Another has come over from the other side of the road to come and be where he is (in the ditch) and like the good Samaritan he has gone that second mile to come where the patient is and to take good care of him.

Yet that is not the last word. Jesus underwent in order that he might overcome. 'I know that my Redeemer lives,' exclaims Job, 'and that at the last day he will stand with me on my side as my advocate.' In the meantime I can dispense then with comforters, advisers, counsellors and even sympathizers — of the wrong kind! I have something infinitely greater than any of them. I have a Saviour who also was brought down and yet who was and is raised up. Thanks be to God who gives us the victory, for (Romans 8:31) 'If God is on our side, who is against us?' Yet none of this was undertaken from condescension but from compassion. The only difference between the good Samaritan and Christ is that he is the companion, physician and patient all in one. He is both the victim and the physician. He bears in his body the marks of the surgeon's wounded hands.

─── Icons and Idols ───

Then the Lord answered Job out of the whirlwind: 'Who is this that darkens counsel by words without knowledge? Gird up your loins like a man, I will question you, and you shall declare to me. Where were you when I laid the foundation of the earth? Tell me, if you have understanding. Who determined its measurements — surely you know! Or who stretched the line upon it? On what were its bases sunk, or who laid its cornerstone, when the morning stars sang together, and all the sons of God shouted for joy?'   Job 38:1−7

His-story God is not answerable to man in the courtroom of earthly justice, where there is an arrogance and pretentiousness in so much of our human vocabulary. God cannot be summoned to speak in the proportions of a man-made witness box. So much of Job's case, as he has presented it, is tailored for that kind of setting, which demands puny explanations to questions of cosmic proportions.

So when finally God speaks for the first time in nearly forty chapters of human rhetoric, he speaks from his divine point of view — the perspective not simply of time, but of eternity; not even only from the perspective of earth, but of space and from the very heart of God himself. From the human point of view, the puny scales of human justice are lost in what the book of Job terms the whirlwind.

That same wind — mighty and rushing that overturns and demolishes the pretentious skyscrapers of human vocabulary — reduces Job's words to dust and brings at last a note of ultimate reality and new proportions to the debate. The word used for 'counsel' in Hebrew means more than haphazard advice such as Job's 'comforters' have given. It suggests rather a large, sweeping plan of consistent and intelligent design. Where on earth is Job in all of that? Scarcely visible is the answer! So again the Hebrew word used for man (*geber*) denotes man in his strength as a warrior and combatant. But look who he is taking on! There is a note here of the absurd as God extends to Job an invitation to debate and combat, which even might begin to take Job seriously.

The Jesus story Yet, strangely, God has taken man seriously in Jesus. He has entered our environment and proclaimed his 'counsels' in words small enough to be understood by the limits of man's mind. He has entered history by emptying himself. What was hidden has been revealed; what was disguised has been disclosed. And all of this is what we mean by the greatest absurdity of all — the incarnation, namely, that God has not simply come down to our level to tease us but rather has become as we are in order that we may ultimately become as he is. We cannot hope that it can all make sense — not common sense, that is. It is not such a common and straightforward matter as that. God impacted history, but that was not the end of the story. By history's taking on eternity, the water of reason, human justice and common sense became wine of that most explosive and dangerous vintage — a new wine requiring new bottles. Vision of God's truth and justice demands a new mind-set altogether.

My story All theology — even the most orthodox and proper theology — must only get two cheers! We cannot and we must not try to make God in our own image. We will be given by grace certain insights because men and women of faith always have been given such insights. Yet at best they are only icons. We must never allow them to become idols.

The counsels of the church must be illuminated by God's eternal counsels. In this world, it will not quite add up or make sense — not because good theology is nonsense, but because it is so much more than just common sense. Hence the orthodox Christians of the east have consistently balanced dogmatic theology with apophatic theology. This kind of theology insists on declaring what God is *not* as the sure way of saying what he is. We need to balance the prayer of words with the prayer of silence; our intellectual discussion about the Truth with that discernment of the Truth which alone comes through worship and adoration. Job is moving slowly in that direction — through his passion to glory; through a sense of alienation and isolation into reconciliation. For to be a good theologian is to be a person of prayer. Belief and worship belong together and both alike are best expressed when together with Job on his garbage heap and Jesus in Gethsemane, we have been brought to our knees. We can never make sense of all this until we enter the sanctuary, prostrate in worship and adoration.

Getting What We Deserve?

After the Lord had spoken these words to Job, the Lord said to Eliphaz the Temanite: 'My wrath is kindled against you and against your two friends; for you have not spoken of me what is right, as my servant Job has. Now therefore take seven bulls and seven rams, and go to my servant Job, and offer up for yourselves a burnt offering; and my servant Job shall pray for you, for I will accept his prayer not to deal with you according to your folly; for you have not spoken of me what is right, as my servant Job has.' So Eliphaz the Temanite and Bildad the Shuhite and Zophar the Naamathite went out and did what the Lord had told them; and the Lord accepted Job's prayer.

Job 42:7–9

His-story Eliphaz, Bildad and Zophar had better look out — especially the former! So much of what they had been saying suggested that Job had got what he deserved. Self-made men always want justice without mercy — or so they claim. Chapter one of the old Israel sought rightly to establish the law with a strong sense of the judgement of God. That was important. It still is important — that is, as far as it goes. The trouble is that it does not go far enough. By the end of the Old Testament the limitations of the law, in all its minutiae, are becoming more and more obvious and not least in the laboratory of innocent suffering — undeserved suffering. Clearly people do not get what they deserve — thank God. Is that because some get more grief than they deserve, while happily Eliphaz, Bildad and Zophar and a whole host of others like them do not get what they deserve?

Yet notice that although God instructs Job's comforters to offer sacrifice, he has no need to instruct Job to pray for his friends. Furthermore, although God tells Eliphaz and his companions to fulfil the law and offer sacrifices accordingly, what actually will tip the scales and be effective is that quality of prayer which can only come from the broken heart of Job. 'A broken and contrite heart, O God, thou shalt not despise' (Psalm 51:17). There is no substitute for the sacrifice of the heart. The law and legal rectitude are not enough — eventually only the broken heart of God can open wide enough to embrace the whole of mankind. The sacrifices of the law are simply not enough.

The Jesus story So Jesus goes on where the law leaves off. Jesus did not get what he deserved on Calvary Hill, neither did Barabbas. What happened on that occasion was far from fair. Jesus stood in for Barabbas and got what he (Barabbas) deserved. Barabbas got off the hook and hopefully by three o'clock on Good Friday afternoon was no longer on Calvary Hill. Perhaps he was buying drinks all round at the 'local' back in Jerusalem!

Yet someone has to pay the bill. It's not fair! Free drinks all round? Fifty, sixty, seventy (whatever the number) — all for the price of one? Yes, because one has paid the price for all. J-shaped people, like Job, and in the end of course like Jesus — always stand in for others. They are priests, like Aaron, who enter the sanctuary on behalf of others with the signs and wounds of the other tribes on the ephod of suffering over their hearts. J-shaped people are, or should be, natural intercessors (like Job) who go before the judge daily to plead (not their own cause) but rather the causes of others who cannot or who will not learn to pray.

Christianity does not explain suffering, but it does show us one way of using it for others in the mysterious and loving purposes of God. Suffering is the yeast of intercession, which is not so much a way of prayer as a whole new way of life. In that new life, judgement is balanced with mercy and the law is balanced with grace.

My story Thank God I do *not* get what I deserve. Thank God for the prayers of others (other J-shaped people) and supremely of course for the prayers of Jesus on Calvary Hill. Only so are the sins of Eliphaz, Bildad and Zophar to be forgiven. Only so are we to be delivered from the wrath of God and presented sinless before the throne of grace. Old people, bed-ridden people, paralysed and shut-ins — Job and all the other J-shaped people — please pray for us! St Monica did not only give her life to pray for her son's conversion. She lived her prayer to such an extent that when Augustine was converted she had nothing left to live for. She died and lived her prayer.

Seeing is Believing

Then Job answered the Lord: 'I know that thou canst do all things, and that no purpose of thine can be thwarted. "Who is this that hides counsel without knowledge?" Therefore I have uttered what I did not understand, things too wonderful for me, which I did not know. "Hear, and I will speak; I will question you, and you declare to me." I had heard of thee by the hearing of the ear, but now my eye sees thee; therefore I despise myself, and repent in dust and ashes'. . . . And the Lord restored the fortunes of Job, when he had prayed for his friends; and the Lord gave Job twice as much as he had before. . . And after this Job lived a hundred and forty years, and saw his sons, and his sons' sons, four generations. And Job died, an old man, and full of days.   Job 42:1−6, 10, 16−17

His-story Job is no longer the self-made man. 'The Lord restored the fortunes of Job.' Downcast, Job is now raised up. The old Job was finished; the new Job has only just begun. No birth trauma could be worse than what he has been through — it is as though he has been born again, with the whole of his life ahead of him now. Three score years and ten was a normal span of life, for self-made men. The writer of Job is at pains to tell us that the Lord gave 'twice as much' to Job as he had before. Hence we are told, he lived another one hundred and forty years. Even the mathematics tell a story.

As a self-made man he had become rich before his breakdown. Now God has broken through and his new life is enriched immeasurably. Not only does he now have all that he had before, but more besides — so very much more.

Yet notice that this story is not recounted in the old-fashioned mode. That is old and out of date! Job is no superman, superstar or self-styled hero. All that sort of thing belongs back in the ark and back in the days of Samson and Goliath. In Job there are marks of the new humanity, the new creation and the new order. Everything for Job from now on will be clearly and irrefutably gift — grace, the word is the same in meaning and context. So Job had one hundred and forty years of grace — days and months and years just full of it. Before the crash, he was fulfilled, so fulfilled, it was perhaps difficult for anyone to find any space to fill — the sort of person who is 'impossible to shop for' at birthday times or for Christmas. His stocking was always too full! But everything is different now.

The Jesus story Job's story is very much the shape of things to come according to the teaching of Jesus in the New Testament. 'Seek first the kingdom of God and his righteousness, and all these things shall be yours as well' (Matthew 6:33). 'Truly,' says Jesus, 'I say to you, there is no one who has left house or brothers, or sisters or mother or father or children or lands, for my sake and for the gospel, who will not receive a hundredfold now in this time, houses and brothers and sisters and children and lands, with persecutions, and in the age to come eternal life. But many that are first will be last, and the last first' (Mark 10:29–31). Of course, Job did not choose to lose all; rather, he chose to hold on to God through all and above all. At some point in the journey he simply could not have continued to grow up if he had not let go. The doorway (or the gate) to eternal or real life is simply too narrow to take any more than just the outline and profile of yourself through it. The rest of the baggage cannot go. We all have to pass through the sieve of God's particular love for us. In the kingdom it is always this different way round. You keep what goes through and you can afford to throw away the rest.

My story The turning point for Job was when there was nothing left except Job — those were the real years for Job. Yet in those grace-filled years (a hundred and forty of them) after the crash, he was full of days, full of light. Hollowed out and emptied out from all substitutes, through his Passion and suffering it was possible now to see right through this former man of substance. Even his religion perhaps had been part of what he had acquired — second-hand, along with all the other baggage. But now he no longer relied on the reports and opinions of others: he had seen for himself the light. It was the same light that had seen right through him. No, Job was no hero of *the* faith, but rather a faithful saint. Saints are never self-made. Before the crash he was a good egg — good that is for nothing in particular and everything in general. Then he was broken open.

Now he is not so much good as holy. Holy Job! Holy Job is so much more attractive, than the good old Job who went into hospital! But then good patients are the raw material of which saints are made.

JEREMIAH: THE WITNESS

It's that man again!
It was a cold December day in the year of 604 BC (Jeremiah 36:9). King Jehoiakim, in the fifth year of his reign, sat heavy-hearted, warming himself beside the red and glowing coals of his brazier in the royal palace in Jerusalem. The political and international struggles of his day played heavily upon his mind. The fragile kingdom of Judah over which he ruled was caught in the crossfire between the great imperial powers which surrounded it on every side. Jehoiakim's father — Josiah — had put up a brave fight only five years earlier at Megiddo against the Egyptian empire which under Necho was threatening to take over the remnant of the crumbling Assyrian empire. Jehoiakim in fact owed the throne in no small way to Necho who insisted upon placing him as the somewhat puppet king in Judah.

However, only twelve months earlier, Nebuchadrezzar, the crown prince of Babylon, had routed Necho's forces at Carchemish and clearly for those with eyes to see it would not be long before the imperialistic thrust of the rising empire of Babylon would conquer the kingdom of Judah. Surely the only hope for Judah was to enter into alliance with Egypt and the surrounding countries. That seemed the logical way. That seemed to be in the best interests of the kingdom of Judah.

At that moment, led by Jehudi, the son of Nethaniah, a bunch of government officials burst into the king's chamber. Only that very day a scribe named Baruch had practically caused a riot by standing in the Temple precincts reading a scroll of prophecy. When questioned about the origins of its contents, Baruch had told his enquirers quite openly that the scroll had been dictated by no less a person than Jeremiah the prophet.

'O No — not that man again!' was probably the retort of the king. Was he not already under house-arrest and forbidden to open his mouth? For over twenty years, Jeremiah had prophesied unsettling prophecies to the people and all of them were contrary to the government's policy. Back in the days of Josiah he had been opposing all alliance with Egypt, and had insisted upon recalling Judah to a renewal of faith and witness and justice. Furthermore he had forewarned the people of an ultimate catastrophe — the total destruction of Jerusalem and the Temple by the Babylonian empire. This man must be silenced once and for all.

'Go and fetch the scroll and bring it here, Jehudi,' exclaimed the king (36:21). The scroll was brought. As its words were read the king took his penknife and tore off the columns as each one was spoken. He tossed the torn parchment piece by piece into the fire of the nearby brazier. Some of the men urged the king not to burn the scroll, but he refused to listen and finally the scroll of prophecies was a heap of dust and ashes. But that was not the end of the matter.

Baruch had joined Jeremiah in hiding. It was not long before the prophet took a fresh scroll and re-wrote all the words that had been burned by the king and added some other words besides. To this day we can read these words in the first twenty-five chapters of the book of the prophet Jeremiah.

Suffering, witness and martyrdom

The day of destruction foretold by Jeremiah approached, just eighteen years later — 586 BC. By this time alliances with Egypt and the surrounding countries had proved to be disastrous. Zedekiah, who had succeeded Jehoiakim, was very much the puppet of the pro-Egyptian party at court and as such prevaricated — torn first in this and then in that direction (Jeremiah 38:5, 10). Jeremiah came out of hiding to face angry mobs opposing all alliance with Egypt as he spoke. He prophesied inevitable and ultimate defeat but he also called bravely for spiritual renewal and a new inner commitment of heart, mind and will to the ways of Yahweh. Not unnaturally he was thrown into prison for his message. He was flogged, put into the stocks and finally thrust down into a muddy cistern where he was left to die either of starvation or to be drowned in the mud during the siege of Jerusalem. However a sympathetic negro — an Ethiopian — engineered his removal from the pit. Jeremiah saw the city and the Temple he loved destroyed. He and his scribe Baruch were compelled to accompany the hoards of refugees to Egypt where the story of his brave life and heroic witness ends. The prophet's correspondence with his fellow exiles in Babylon, nevertheless, contains hope, foreseeing a day when the Lord would restore his people back in their own land (Jeremiah 30:10—22). Tradition tells us that Jeremiah was stoned to death by his own people at Tahpanhes, only some five years after the fall of Jerusalem.

Of all the major prophets in the Old Testament, Jeremiah stands out as the most Christ-like in his suffering, his deep love and passion for Jerusalem, its Temple and its religion. He was supremely the J-shaped prophet and the gospel accounts in the New Testament make it clear how very closely Jesus identified himself with Jeremiah's prophetic ministry. Jeremiah was the prophet of the heart — of passion and compassion. Yet he retained a deep faith and trust in God's vindication. We plumb the depths in Jeremiah and we look to the heights with a faith which is clearly nothing less than a resurrection faith in a God of power and righteousness. That faith reaches in Jeremiah deeply into the heart and life of each believer. Quite rightly the church during the liturgy of Holy Week draws deeply upon the well of Jeremiah's teachings, his life and the lamentations in the book which follows the book of Jeremiah. Although the book of Lamentations was almost certainly not from the pen of Jeremiah, nevertheless it closely expresses the grief and experience of the prophet in exile and in the days immediately following the destruction of Jerusalem.

Questions for Discussion and Reflection

1. What is the difference between 'revival' and 'renewal'? Distinguish between the revival of Lazarus and the resurrection of Jesus.

2. Why is there no temple in the heavenly Jerusalem according to the book of Revelation?

3. Why could Jeremiah have such hope for the future? How can we? Is it escapism — if not, why not?

The Way Through

The words of Jeremiah, the son of Hilkiah, of the priests who were in Anathoth in the land of Benjamin, to whom the word of the Lord came in the days of Josiah the son of Amon, king of Judah, in the thirteenth year of his reign. . . Now the word of the Lord came to me saying, 'Before I formed you in the womb I knew you, and before you were born I consecrated you; I appointed you a prophet to the nations.' Then I said, 'Ah, Lord God! Behold, I do not know how to speak, for I am only a youth.' But the Lord said to me, 'Do not say, "I am only a youth"; for to all to whom I send you you shall go, and whatever I command you you shall speak. Be not afraid of them, for I am with you to deliver you, says the Lord.' Then the Lord put forth his hand and touched my mouth; and the Lord said to me, 'Behold, I have put my words in your mouth. See, I have set you this day over nations and over kingdoms, to pluck up and to break down, to destroy and to overthrow, to build and to plant.'   Jeremiah 1:1–10

His-story 'In my beginning is my end' (T. S. Eliot). Jeremiah's identity originated in the mind and will of God. His vocation did not begin at some point when he qualified to be a prophet. It began not in Anathoth (Anata) just three miles north of Jerusalem. It began before time in the mind of the Creator. Jeremiah had no worldly qualifications. At the time of his conscious call (627 BC) he was still 'only a youth'. Furthermore he was not eloquent, nor had he any formal training in rhetoric. How could he possibly set himself up as some kind of self-made prophet? Surely such achievements call for an impressive, pure, king-like leader with the political skills of a warrior — to pluck up and break down kingdoms? In what way then could Jeremiah possibly respond to such a call? It was a tall order by any standards.

The Jesus story 'Are you a king?', Pilate was to ask Jesus only a few days after the prophet from Nazareth had entered Jerusalem riding on an ass. The whole procession had constituted rather a pathetic bunch of people who littered his path with palm branches and shouted out a sort of kingly greeting: Hosanna!

We need to know, not merely geographically but certainly in every other way, the route that Jesus took into Jerusalem on Palm Sunday. In the first place it was no way for an earthly king to ride. It was J-shaped! Jesus does not exactly cut the figure of a successful, worldly warrior seated on an ass. The whole scene is much like that foretold by that other Old Testament prophet: 'Tell the daughter of Zion, behold, your king is coming to you, humble and mounted on an ass, and on a colt, the foal of an ass' (Isaiah 62:11, Zechariah 9:9). A king? Surely you have to be joking!

Later the same week Thomas was to ask Jesus how it was possible for those who wanted to be disciples and to follow in the way of Jesus to know the journey, the road and the way to go. Later still it was the same doubting Thomas whom Jesus invited to touch the marks of the nails in his risen body as evidence that the risen Jesus was indeed the selfsame person who had been crucified only three days earlier. 'The way, Thomas, is the way of the nails.' The way to Jerusalem — that true Jerusalem which is above — is the way of the nails.

The journey of Holy Week is J-shaped. It begins with a contradiction and ends with a contradiction. It is *the* way to glory and a kingdom, but as Jesus tells Pilate neither that kingdom nor that glory are of this world. The kingdoms of this world have to be plucked up and broken down, destroyed and overthrown in order that they can be rebuilt upon eternal and unshakeable foundations. The journey of Holy Week is the journey to that kind of kingdom and Jesus is that kind of king. We must not get all carried away on Palm Sunday and mistake it for either the end or the beginning; rather, it is the beginning of the end of all things. The beginning of all this was before the earthly birth of Jesus (like the vocation of Jeremiah). It originated in the very heart of God himself.

My story   Bishop Michael Ramsey used to remind us that the journey of Jesus back to the light and to the Father and his journey into the world with its darkness and pain were one and the same journey. Union with the Father is the *other* side of Jerusalem, pain and darkness. Jesus commits us to undertake that same single journey. The way on a map is from Bethany into Jerusalem, *through* the scourging and the mocking, along the Via Dolorosa, *through* crucifixion outside the far wall of the city and then on to another village, Emmaus beyond the city. The journey is *through* the world and back to the Father. It is not a straight ascending course to a God who is out of touch with the scars and wounds of the world. Rather it is a journey into and through the world, finally transcending the kingdoms and pretentions of this world and bringing us into full and eternal communion with God the Father.

'Ride on! ride on in majesty!
In lowly pomp ride on to die;
Bow thy meek head to mortal pain,
Then take, O God, thy power, and reign.'
(Henry Milman)

Man-made or God-given?

The word that came to Jeremiah from the Lord: 'Stand in the gate of the Lord's house, and proclaim there this word, and say, Hear the word of the Lord, all you men of Judah who enter these gates to worship the Lord. Thus says the Lord of hosts, the God of Israel, Amend your ways and your doings, and I will let you dwell in this place. Do not trust in these deceptive words: "This is the temple of the Lord, the temple of the Lord, the temple of the Lord".' . . . 'Behold, you trust in deceptive words to no avail. Will you steal, murder, commit adultery, swear falsely, burn incense to Baal, and go after other gods that you have not known, and then come and stand before me in this house, which is called by my name, and say, "We are delivered!" — only to go on doing all these abominations? Has this house, which is called by my name, become a den of robbers in your eyes? Behold, I myself have seen it, says the Lord.'

Jeremiah 7:1−4, 8−11

His-story At the heart of the religion of the old Israel was the Temple with its worship and sacrifices. Yet Jeremiah is impelled by Yahweh to get to the heart of it all. He is told to go and stand 'in the gate of the Lord's house' and point the people of God beyond the religion of the Temple (which was to be destroyed in any case in the sack of Jerusalem by Nebuchadrezzar in 586 BC). For if at the heart of Jerusalem was the Temple, then at the heart of temple worship must be a heart of faith and loving obedience. 'The Temple of the Lord', with its sacrifices and festivals, was of course the pride of Jerusalem. Intended by God to be the focus of a worship which transcended the physical stones of a building, instead the Temple and its worship had become not so much an icon as an idol. So the Temple was abused by the worship which had ceased to command the hearts and wills of God's people. God's house had become a den of robbers used for the selfish ends of national pride and a man-made religion. To the cult of the Temple and worship with its strong national and corporate identity, Jeremiah must bring the sword of the word of God. This would inevitably be painful, unpopular and costly — not least for the prophet himself.

The Jesus story Between Palm Sunday and Maundy Thursday we are led to believe in the gospels that Jesus spent the night in the home of friends at Bethany just outside Jerusalem. Each day he went into the city to the heart of Jerusalem, to the Temple, and so to the heart of his message. So the Word of God (Jesus) enters the Temple at the climax of his challenge. (The chronology of this is not important. In St John's gospel the cleansing of the Temple occurs at the outset of the ministry of Jesus while in the Synoptic gospels it occurs in the final chapters. Both records are saying the same thing: the heart of the message of Jesus is his challenge to the worship and cult of the Temple. Things that are of first importance are either at the outset — 'first things first' — or at the climax. It depends how you see it.)

Jesus enters the Temple and opens it up, clearing space for the Word of God to ventilate the gloomy sanctuaries with God's call to the heart and to the will. He weeps over the city and recalls God's people to the need to find deeper and more secure and lasting foundations for their faith. These must rest not on man-made institutions and organizations, but on nothing less than a personal faith in Christ — whose body is to be the new Temple. In AD 70 the Temple of Christ's day was razed to the ground by the Romans and utterly destroyed.

My story The church is primarily an organism before it is an organization. It is the Body of Christ. Its foundations rest upon faith in Christ, the Lord of history. No other foundations have we than those which have 'already been laid', says St Paul, 'even Jesus Christ' (1 Corinthians 3:11).

The living church is to be found at that point where word and worship converge: scripture and sacrament belong together. Only so are we recalled to real renewal. The temples of a religion of our own devising have to be overthrown many times before the temple of living faith, obedient prayer and costly worship can be truly established.

'The dearest idol I have known,
Whate'er that idol be,
Help me to tear it from thy throne,
And worship only thee.'

(William Cowper)

Second-best or First-hand?

The word that came to Jerusalem from the Lord: 'Arise, and go down to the potter's house, and there I will let you hear my words.' So I went down to the potter's house, and there he was working at his wheel. And the vessel he was making of clay was spoiled in the potter's hand, and he reworked it into another vessel, as it seemed good to the potter to do.

Then the word of the Lord came to me: 'O house of Israel, can I not do with you as this potter has done? says the Lord. Behold, like the clay in the potter's hand, so are you in my hand, O house of Israel.'

Jeremiah 18:1—6

His-story   Actions speak louder than words. Every picture tells a story. God's word in the Old Testament is seldom abstract. It is generally enfleshed in events, signs and symbols. The prophets of the Old Testament are not like abstract philosophers with long beards. They are always where the action is — the divine action and interaction.

What is happening at the potter's wheel highlights the divine desire to refashion, remake and renew mankind. Jeremiah was not a pessimist. He was pointing to the only source of real hope for the world — the re-creation of the universe at the hands of a loving and holy God. His refusal to accept second-best or to settle for a compromise of expediency, gives the illusion of a negative outlook. Sometimes we have to say an immediate 'No' in order to say an ultimate 'Yes'.

The Jesus story   On one of his visits to the Temple and Jerusalem during Holy Week, Jesus passes a fig tree which failed to bear fruit. He points to that fig tree as a sign of life which has refused renewal and fruitfulness. The tree withers dramatically before the eyes of the astonished disciples (Mark 11:12—21).

Calvary Hill is the anvil of the universe, as central to God's ultimate design as the wheel for the potter in Jeremiah's experience. The former design of the universe through one man's disobedience, has rendered that plan fruitless and barren. But now there is a new opportunity, for the former things are passing away — this is the message of Jesus. He summons the whole creation to come out of the tombs and prisons of our own making and to appropriate the new design of God who is also entering the world through one Man. This time, however, it is the obedience of one Man which is the door for God's future to enter our present. The challenge of the new is always relevant and contemporary: 'Today, when you hear his voice, do not harden your hearts' (Hebrews 3:7—8); 'Then I said, "Lo, I have come to do thy will, O God" ' (Hebrews 10:7).

My story 'Behold, I make all things new.' That promise of the last book of the Bible, shows us the point of all life and the point of history. Breaking into history in the person of Jesus is the promise of hope — in the design of a new humanity: 'a new heaven and a new earth' (Revelation 21:1).

But notice that the challenge of life is to be found in God's gift to us of what is new. That is neither the same as the contemporary on the one hand nor 'the good old days' on the other hand. It is neither a glorification of the present, the past or the future. It is something much more radical than that.

Nevertheless, the flaws of the old life can most certainly be brought into the new, but only *through* the fire. There is continuity with the former design, but only after a real break with the past in order to make way for that radical re-designing which is always the other side of 'death'. After all, who wants 'seconds' when the new is being held out?

Furthermore, all this is a gift demanding only that we accept it with gratitude. Real life — new life; life in all its fullness — is beginning now for all those who see in the suffering, death and resurrection of Jesus the shape of things to come. The face of God's future for all of us is a new profile in which we can just still recognize something of the marks and scars of the old. 'Grace perfects nature,' insists Aquinas. For at last we shall be 'all there' and 'together' ('all things are ours') with our resurrection body which after all looks what it is and is what it seems — the new creation. For 'if any one is in Christ', then he or she can be nothing less than 'a new creation' (2 Corinthians 5:17).

Lowest Ebb

> How lonely sits the city that was full of people! How like a widow she has become, she that was great among the nations! She that was a princess among the cities has become a vassal. She weeps bitterly in the night, tears on her cheeks; among all her lovers she has none to comfort her; all her friends have dealt treacherously with her, they have become her enemies. . . Jerusalem remembers in the days of her affliction and bitterness all the precious things that were hers from days of old. When her people fell into the hand of the foe, and there was none to help her, the foe gloated over her, mocking at her downfall. . . 'Is it nothing to you, all you who pass by? Look and see if there is any sorrow like my sorrow which was brought upon me. . .'
>
> Lamentations 1:1−2, 7, 12a

His-story The book of Lamentations is closely associated with Jeremiah because it clearly stands at the same sort of turning point in history as the catastrophic events of Jeremiah's day. Most probably its historical background is also the fall of Jerusalem in 586 BC.

As we have seen, the journey or passage into new life is never quite straightforward. There is a sense in which all *our* hopes must first be cast down before we are raised up to a new life and real hope. We reach some sort of turning point, but not until we have gone a long way 'down'.

In this passage we see Jerusalem at its lowest and inevitably in the vale of tears. Tears and baptism belong together — we are baptized in water. That water is essentially the tears of God from the Passion of Christ.

All who are on the road to new life have at some point reached this turning point. At the same time all our hope seems to be in the past as we reminisce with nostalgia about a glory which has departed. 'Jerusalem remembers in the days of her affliction and bitterness all the precious things that were hers from days of old.'

In our depression and desolation the golden age appears to be in the past. On the way 'up' however everything is in reverse. Our hope is the future. The best is yet to come. In Christ, things past and things future are all ours in time present.

The Jesus story 'And when he drew near and saw the city (Jerusalem) he wept over it, saying, "Would that even today you knew the things that make for peace! But now they are hid from your eyes. For the days shall come upon you, when your enemies will cast up the bank about you and surround you, and hem you in on every side, and dash you to the ground. . . because you did not know the time of your visitation" ' (Luke 19:41—44). So what will be raised up in the place of Jerusalem? Some poor substitute? What of the Temple? The prophecy foretold by Jesus occurred historically in AD 70 and to our day, devout Jews stand by the 'Wailing Wall' of the former temple, which no longer exists, and they weep and wail for 'the glory that has departed'.

In place of the old, God has raised up the new. Nevertheless the new is not a substitute or poor second-best for the old. It is the other way round. God has raised us from the old Jerusalem to the new heavenly Jerusalem where there is no need of a temple. St John is adamant that when Jesus spoke of a new temple he spoke of his own body. 'Jesus answered them, "Destroy this temple, and in three days I will raise it up". The Jews then said, "It has taken forty-six years to build this temple, and will you raise it up in three days?" But he spoke of the temple of his body' (John 2:19—21).

The real temple and the real people of Israel have replaced the old shadows. We are not left with tears only of nostalgia, with our hope locked in the past. This is now reversed. Our hope lies in the future and already as members of the Body of Christ we have a foretaste of the real joy, love and worship of the heavenly Jerusalem — the Jerusalem which is above, which is the mother of us all. There are still tears, but now tears of anticipation.

My story The pagan world looked back to the past to its glory and the golden age. It spoke of the 'good old days' — a very pagan phrase indeed. Since the resurrection, and because of the resurrection, all this is reversed. God has kept the 'good wine' until now and the best for the future — the true golden age, the reign of God. In that day all things will be consummated in Christ and all things will be ours for we are his and he is God's. Anticipation has replaced lamentation. Such is the Christian view of history and the Christian grounds for hope — a hope which cannot be taken away.

Gospel of Service

So they took Jeremiah and cast him into the cistern of Malchiah, the king's son, which was in the court of the guard, letting Jeremiah down by ropes. And there was no water in the cistern, but only mire, and Jeremiah sank in the mire. When Ebedmelech the Ethiopian, a eunuch, who was in the king's house, heard that they had put Jeremiah into the cistern — the king was sitting in the Benjamin Gate — Ebedmelech went from the king's house and said to the king, 'My lord the king, these men have done evil in all that they did to Jeremiah the prophet by casting him into the cistern; and he will die there of hunger, for there is no bread left in the city.' Then the king commanded Ebedmelech, the Ethiopian, 'Take three men with you from here, and lift Jeremiah the prophet out of the cistern before he dies.' So Ebedmelech took the men with him and went to the house of the king, to a wardrobe of the storehouse, and took from there old rags and worn-out clothes, which he let down to Jeremiah in the cistern by ropes. Then Ebedmelech the Ethiopian said to Jeremiah, 'Put the rags and clothes between your armpits and the ropes.' Jeremiah did so. Then they drew Jeremiah up with ropes and lifted him out of the cistern. And Jeremiah remained in the court of the guard.   Jeremiah 38:6—13

His-story Jeremiah the outcast is cast down into the cistern in isolation and degradation. Ebedmelech, the Ethiopian, a eunuch, and therefore in many ways an outcast, goes to the king on behalf of Jeremiah. He pleads Jeremiah's cause and intercedes for him. Ebedmelech was a displaced person who could sympathize with Jeremiah, reaching out and reaching down to the prophet in his time of need and in his hour of desolation. It is frequently the outcast who can minister best to the downcast.

The Jesus story 'In saying "He ascended," what does it mean but that he also descended into the lower parts of the earth? He who descended is he who also ascended far above all the heavens, that he might fill all things' (Ephesians 4:9—10). Christ's journey of Holy Week runs the full gamut. It is a single journey — the journey back to the Father and the fullness of life in the communion of the Spirit.

So on Maundy Thursday night, Jesus spends some part of that night in the prison in the house of Caiaphas. Modern archaeology can take us almost to the very spot and to the place of the dungeon in which Jesus was cast down. It is in the lower parts of that house of Caiaphas, after he had been flogged, tortured and tormented that we see Jesus on Maundy Thursday night. Along with Jeremiah and all the other J-shaped people, the journey of Jesus home to God takes a similar direction. Is it too much to suppose that on Good Friday, words from the Psalms flooded from the subconscious into the conscious — some of the words of the psalms of 'descent'?

'I waited patiently for the Lord,' is the song of a heart that has hit rock bottom. Yet even the Psalms are J-shaped. Often if they begin with a sense of desolation and isolation as in Psalm 22 (My God, my God, why hast thou forsaken me?) they nearly always end on an 'ascending' note. Psalm 22 ends at precisely that point and it is significant that we hear the opening words of that Psalm on the lips of Jesus in his agony on the cross. Sometimes the very stitching of the fabric of the Psalm is J-shaped throughout. For they are words on the lips of a people whose lives and stories are shaped in the same way.

'I waited patiently for the Lord;
he inclined to me and heard my cry.
He drew me up from the desolate pit,
out of the miry bog,
and set my feet upon a rock,
making my steps secure.
He put a new song in my mouth,
a song of praise to our God.'
(Psalm 40:1−3)

My story It is, as we saw, so often the displaced person — the outcast — who goes out of his way to raise up the downcast. Ebedmelech the Ethiopian came to the help of Jeremiah. Simon of Cyrene, coming in from the 'outside', is compelled to carry the cross of Jesus. The colour of their skins (they were probably both black) is not our prime concern. As outcasts, both were compelled and impelled by different forces to come to where the need was. Only a J-shaped person can really help others at that turning point. The Good Samaritan is no idle invention: as an outcast he identifies with the outcasts. They must weep with those who weep and rejoice with those that rejoice.

Maundy Thursday is the day we celebrate the new commandment — to love each other as God loves us. Head over heels, Jesus the Lord and servant washes the bruises and sores of our feet, wounded by the stones and pitfalls of the same journey and the same life. Jesus the outcast comes down to where we are in order to raise us up to where he is. The gospel of glory and the gospel of service are one and the same gospel — a J-shaped gospel throughout.

GOOD FRIDAY

He Stooped to Conquer

I am the man who has seen affliction under the rod of his wrath; he has driven and brought me into darkness without any light; surely against me he turns his hand again and again the whole day long. He has made my flesh and my skin waste away, and broken my bones; he has besieged and enveloped me with bitterness and tribulation; he has made me dwell in darkness like the dead of long ago. . . He drove into my heart the arrows of his quiver; I have become the laughing stock of all peoples, the burden of their songs all day long. He has filled me with bitterness, he has sated me with wormwood. . . Remember my affliction and my bitterness, the wormwood and the gall! *Lamentations 3:1—6, 13—19*

His-story After the fall of Jerusalem in 586 BC, many Jews were carried off into exile. Jeremiah suffered with them all the way. Tradition tells us that when some of the exiles returned later, Jeremiah met a martyr's death by stoning.

The record of the true prophets throughout history is not a happy one. The world has variously, 'taken one, beaten one, stoned one and killed another'. To live the life of truth and to witness to God's love in the straight ascending course of an obedient life, naturally goes against the grain of the world. Too much truth, too much love, too much beauty always 'threatens' the world. Threatened men are frightened men; fearful men are cruel and destructive.

Sin is not so much that we go too far, but that we conspire not to go far enough. The true prophets always went too far in their witness to truth and love. In the end, almost inevitably the witness is therefore also the martyr.

The Jesus story 'I will send my beloved son; it may be they will respect him' (Luke 20:13). Jesus is God's way of being human but he is all too much. The light of his love is all too much for us to bear. Children are frequently afraid of the dark, but more often grownups are afraid of the light. 'This is the judgement, that light has entered the world and men prefer darkness' (John 3:19). So before Herod and Pilate, the lawyers and the religious men pervert the truth. Then the soldiers in their turn inevitably disfigure Christ's face. Truth and beauty belong together. In refuting the one we inevitably disfigure the other. Then they lead Jesus out to crucify him, nailing his body in the sort of shape which finally renders it impotent. Then they let him die.

The trouble was that he had gone too far. If only he could have settled for quite good things and not always wanted to witness to the best — God's best. He might have lived a long and useful life, this side of death. The trouble was he went too far!

Truth to tell he went all the way in fact. He went from heaven to earth and hell and back again as the laser beam of God's total love and light. As such he is *the* witness to *the* ultimate truth — that love which is stronger than death and which alone can break through the barrier of sin and alienation into union and communion with the source of love — God himself. 'The light shines in the darkness'. . . 'There was darkness over the whole land from the sixth to the ninth hour.'

My story The cross within us is that place where light and darkness converge in conflict and contradiction. There is a part of us which is even now ready to shout, 'Hosanna to the king!' There is also another part which is compelled to shout, 'Crucify!' However loudly we strike these dissident notes the echo which ricochets from Calvary Hill is, thank God, a single word, 'Alleluya' — which, spelt out, might well be the first word from the cross: 'Father, forgive them, for they know not what they do.' We must frequently go to the Calvary Hill of the heart and find that cross within us as surely as St Helena did when she so diligently searched around the ancient world for the relics of the true cross from Calvary Hill in Palestine.

'In the cross of Christ I glory' or in Paul's words we must resolve to know only 'Christ and him crucified'. 'Have this mind among yourselves, which is yours in Christ Jesus, who, though he was in the form of God, did not count equality with God a thing to be grasped, but emptied himself, taking the form of a servant, being born in the likeness of men. And being found in human form he humbled himself and became obedient unto death, even death on a cross. Therefore God has highly exalted him and bestowed on him the name which is above every name, that at the name of Jesus every knee should bow, in heaven and on earth and under the earth. . .' (Philippians 2: 5–10). He finally stoops to conquer. Perhaps, after all, he is a real king — the true king.

In the Meantime?

'Behold, the days are coming, says the Lord, when I will make a new covenant with the house of Israel and the house of Judah, not like the covenant which I made with their fathers when I took them by the hand to bring them out of the land of Egypt, my covenant which they broke, though I was their husband, says the Lord. But this is the covenant which I will make with the house of Israel after those days, says the Lord: I will put my law within them, and I will write it upon their hearts; and I will be their God, and they shall be my people. And no longer shall each man teach his neighbour and each his brother, saying, "Know the Lord," for they shall all know me, from the least of them to the greatest, says the Lord; for I will forgive their iniquity, and I will remember their sin no more.' Jeremiah 31:31–34

His-story For the other exiles in Babylon, Jeremiah nevertheless prophesies hope — hope of restoration and return to Jerusalem and the Temple. For Jeremiah the best he could hope for was the *revival* of God's ancient people: that in some way they would come back to life and to their former life in Jerusalem in the days of Ezra and Nehemiah with the rebuilding of the city and the restoration of the Temple.

The Jesus story Jesus did not come back to life — he went all the way *through* life and *through* death and was raised to new and fuller life in union and communion with the Father. Wherever we have drawn lines of alienation and separation this side of the grave or the other, Jesus draws another line right through. That constitutes a cross — the significant sign of infinite and unconditional love.

Tradition in the church teaches that on this day Jesus descended into hell. Yet 'hell' (like heaven in reverse) is not primarily a question of altitude, but rather of attitude. Hell is that place or state of unloving or partial, conditional love — on my terms. It is as though Jesus 'spent Holy Saturday' (an obviously unfortunate turn of phrase) 'preaching' to and calling out to all who have gone before with their imperfect, unfulfilled vision of God and his unconditional love. Sin is imperfect loving. Imperfect love (in the name of the good things of life — law, religion, politics or marriage) will always go so far and then draw back, drawing a line of separation: 'Love bade me welcome, but my soul drew back' (George Herbert).

Jesus insists, however, on going all the way down (or across, depending on how you see it) to the opposite of God in order to call the opposite pole of loving into union with himself and therefore ultimately with the Father. That union is always the *other side* of sin, fear and death. Jesus as a pioneer is the first through that barrier of sin — the first through the death barrier.

My story 'If you get there before I do, just bore a hole and pull me through!', we might well sing. Jesus, as the pioneer of love perfected, draws passengers (or even parasites) through the hoop after him. Humanity can at last be at home with God (heaven) providing we have the right attitude (not so much altitude). That attitude is to love with the love we have been loved with (cp. 1 John 4). It is the love of costly covenant not cautious contract. We do not need to try to pull ourselves up by our own boot-strings after all — but rather, to know we are loved — even '*in extremis*'!

The new life begins when we know we are loved: infinite eternal life begins when we know we are loved infinitely and eternally in a covenant which cannot be broken — at least from God's side. That is real security.

It began in my baptism. So in the vigil before the resurrection morning, as the church recalls that radical breakthrough of history, we re-affirm our baptismal vows. Marked for life, with the sign of that cross, the rest of life is a journey of discovery — discovering what it really means to be loved infinitely and responding to that incredible gift. That is *real* security, which should mean that I never need to feel threatened again. That is heaven — union with God — and has nothing necessarily to do with altitude, time or space. The journey of my exodus is the same journey as Jesus took in reverse, from the hell of alienation, through life, through death and back to union with God.

In all of this wonderful transformation, God keeps the initiative. We can only love because we now know (what Jeremiah and all those other

J-shaped people before Christ could not know): that God has first loved us. There is a way back to heaven which passes through wherever we could ever find ourselves (purgatory, hell or any other place). It is not the way we see things normally. Only in Christ do we have the opportunity to see it the right way round: inside out, upside down and head-over-heels *in* love for ever.

EASTER DAY

JESUS AND THE RESURRECTION

——— Blessing in Disguise? ———

And (Jesus) said to them, 'O foolish men, and slow of heart to believe all that the prophets have spoken! Was it not necessary that the Christ should suffer these things and enter into his glory?' And beginning with Moses and all the prophets, he interpreted to them in all the scriptures the things concerning himself.

So they drew near to the village to which they were going. He appeared to be going further, but they constrained him, saying, 'Stay with us, for it is toward evening and the day is now far spent.' So he went in to stay with them. When he was at the table with them, he took the bread and blessed, and broke it, and gave it to them. And their eyes were opened and they recognized him; and he vanished out of their sight. They said to each other, 'Did not our hearts burn within us while he talked to us on the road, while he opened to us the scriptures?'   Luke 24:25—32

His-story We are not sure where these two disciples were going, because there are at least three possible sites on the map for the village of Emmaus. Perhaps *they* were lost also and were not too sure where they were going! What is quite clear is that they were disillusioned. 'We had hoped,' they say as they break down before the anonymous stranger who draws alongside them on that road to nowhere. They just wanted to get away from it all.

The risen Christ can meet them on the road to nowhere precisely because he has been everywhere — all the way to hell and back again. Jesus has met up with Cleopas and his friend though they do not recognize him for who he is, until he discloses his identity. Resurrection faith comes more from revelation than speculation. The true identity of Jesus Christ is always apparently disguised in order that it may be truly disclosed.

A Bible study ensues. Jesus discloses his identity by identifying with all the other J-shaped people of contradiction from the Old Testament. Surely they will now recognize Christ for who he is and not just for who they might like him to be. So *through* scripture, *through* sacrament and *through* that inner awareness and warming of the Spirit, the penny drops and they make the connection, between things they had always thought were opposites: between suffering and glory; love and vulnerability; sovereignty and service. The road to disclosure and the orthodox is always *through* the way of disguise and paradox. Yet 'X' marks the spot on that map of the heart as the place where three ways meet (scripture, sacrament and Spirit). It is the place of vision and disclosure.

The Jesus story 'I thank thee, Father, Lord of heaven and earth, that thou hast hidden these things from the wise and understanding and revealed them to babes' (Matthew 11:25). Like bad detectives, Cleopas and his friend were looking for all the wrong clues in the wrong places — away from the conflict. They were asking all the wrong questions. The record of J-shaped people's lives teaches us to seek out contradiction and to look for the good news all among the bad. In a sense you have to start at the end to find the real beginning and you have to go to the place of death to find the living. For it is in service that you will find sovereignty and in losing trust in your self-sufficiency that God can give you a living faith in him.

My story As soon as they recognize Jesus they are converted — that is to say they turned round and returned to the place of conflict, fellowship and worship. The resurrection life (the new life) had begun. Everything is now seen the other way round. The last place they ever expected to meet him was the first place they came to know him. Instead of the signs pointing anywhere or nowhere, they all make sense and all roads begin to lead somewhere. Even the light from the moon just rising points the shadows in a helpful direction, disguising what would be distractions and disclosing the next step on the road.

So now, those lost disciples are back on track. But notice how, in the light of J-shaped faith, there is one further feature. For just at the moment of recognition when all the bells began to ring, Jesus vanishes from their sight. The moment they reached for the camera, with the words on their lips, 'Hold it' — he has gone.

Yesterday's disclosure must appear in the clothes of disguise today if it is not to be tomorrow's idolatry. It does not matter how far you go with this Jesus; he always makes as though he would go further. 'There is no stopping place in this life. No, nor was there ever one for any man, no matter how far along the way he has come' (Meister Eckhart).

So with hearts on fire and stout walking-shoes for the road, the disciples of Jesus, as apostles of the risen Lord, set out on the first mission of the church. They will never go home again — well, not *back* home. They are on their way *through* the shadows of their earthly home, to the light and glory of their true home in heaven. There, along with Joel, Jacob, Joshua, Joseph, Jonah, Job, Jeremiah, Paul, Augustine, and all the other J-shaped people of God in Christ, we shall 'be still and see; we shall see and we shall love; we shall love and we shall praise. Behold what will be, in the end, without end! For what is our end, but to reach that kingdom which has no end?' (Augustine, *The City of God*).

The Bible Reading Fellowship was founded 'to encourage the systematic and intelligent reading of the Bible, to emphasize its spiritual message and to take advantage of new light shed on Holy Scripture'.

Over the years the Fellowship has proved a trustworthy guide for those who want an open, informed and contemporary approach to the Bible. It retains a sense of the unique authority of Scripture as a prime means by which God communicates.

As an ecumenical organization, the Fellowship embraces all Christian traditions and its readers are to be found in most parts of the world.